TWO
YOUNG
BOYS

& OTHER STORIES FROM THE LIBERATION STRUGGLE OF SOUTH SUDAN

LINO ANGOK KUEC

he publisher wishes to acknowledge and thank Dr Douglas H. Johnson for his invaluable help and support for Africa World Books and its mission of preserving and promoting African cultural and literary traditions and history. Dr Johnson and fellow historians have been instrumental in ensuring that African people remain connected to their past and their identity. Africa World Books is proud to carry on this mission.

ISBN: 978-0-6455229-8-3

Cover design, typesetting and layout : Africa World Books

Africa
World Books
Pty Ltd

This book is dedicated to all my children
and their mothers, and my grandchildren,
the children of all my sons and daughters
wherever they are.

CONTENTS

ACKNOWLEDGMENTS

My gratitude and many thanks go to my lifetime friends, Associate Professor Stephen Akot Wol and Ustaz Honorable Joseph Ukel Abango. Both have been friends of mine since intermediate school days, Maridi Institute of Education and University of Khartoum. Although they were busy people, they spared the time to go over the manuscript.

The late Joseph was a minister in the government of South Sudan and Stephen an administrator and a lecturer in the University of Bahr el Ghazal. Both read, corrected, deleted and added to the final draft.

My gratitude and thanks also go to my other friend, the late Bol Majok Adiang who was with me when I started writing this piece of work. He was the second dictionary I referred to when I needed some information.

My thanks also go to his son Mariak Bol Majok who found for me a typist and the publisher of the book.

I also thank Acuil Malith Banggol who suggested I contact Peter Lual Reech Deng in Australia to consider publishing my book where other South Sudanese had also had their books published.

Last but not least my gratitude and thanks go to my daughter Ajokdit Lino Angok in Australia who settled the expenses for publishing the book. I would not have been able to pay the bill otherwise.

INTRODUCTION

T his book is my own work. I have written what I thought or remembered. My reference has been a dictionary and at times the late Bol Majok Adiang. The book is mostly fiction but some historical facts and political elements can be found here and there. Some names are of real people I remembered to have done good or bad for the country of South Sudan since the early 1950's up to the time of writing.

The writer is a graduate of the University of Khartoum, Faculty of Arts. He majored in English Literature. He earned a diploma from the University College of Swansea (UK) in development studies. He is a career teacher who taught in elementary schools, secondary schools and the University of Bahr el Ghazal. When he joined the movement, he trained teachers and participated in the preparation of South Sudan's first curriculum. He was in charge of the English panel. He compiled primary school English textbooks. Books 6, 7, and 8 were prepared by him. These books are now being used in South Sudan primary schools.

TWO YOUNG BOYS

CHAPTER ONE

C hance brought the two young boys together. They met casually or by chance. Abdun Kedit was an Agar from Rumbek and Riel Deng, a Twic of Gogrial. The two were under the age of eighteen when they met.

Riel Deng came to Rumbek with an officer, whose company was ordered to reinforce the SPLM forces that had attacked Rumbek Town. Meanwhile, Abdun served another officer in a company which had after a long struggle captured the town of Rumbek. The two young boys became so intimate that each looked for the other when absent. They slept in the same place and ate from the same plate.

It appeared as if the boys grew up together since they were children. An assignment given to one of them was shared by the two. The boys were as friendly as David and Jonathan.

The boys learned a great deal about the use of arms and guns. After the capture of Rumbek by the SPLM forces, there were many abandoned guns, and they were common everywhere in the town. The boys could dismantle and put back the different parts of most of the guns. They also taught themselves how to use different types of guns and how to fire them. While the officers they served were away on operations or training exercises, they stole AK47 automatic rifles and taught themselves marksmanship far from the hearing of the town's people.

They practised aiming accurately at a target, and not to miss it. The boys also practised running fast without stopping or becoming tired quickly. Every time they were alone, they practised overcoming daring obstacles. Each of them tried to outshine the other.

The two could scale any tree, no matter how tall it was, even if it had no branches to catch hold of. They could go for over a day without taking a nap or drinking a cup of water.

Every military exercise the officers and the men did, they did, and they outperformed them. When the soldiers went for military training outside the area, they were prevented from following. However, they practised their own mock attacks and counter attacks.

Abdun Kedit was tall and slender in body and light in

movement. Riel Deng however was rather fat, but light in movement and older than Kedit.

One time the boys went to visit Abdun's village. The village was along a river. Water filled the river throughout the year. There, the two practised swimming. They spent several hours each day in the river, in order to see who the fastest swimmer was. The two passed each other from time to time.

After two months stay they returned to Rumbek to find that the company in which were the officers the boys served was ordered to move to Northern Bahr el Ghazal area. Northern Bahr el Ghazal included Tonj, Gogrial and Aweil, in military terms. The boys did not know which particular area they were to go to first. The company had left a week earlier, before their arrival.

However, Riel was happy. He would take Abdun to visit his home in Twic, even if they went to Aweil area first. It was easy to move from Aweil area to his home. The two packed the things left behind by the officers and went after them. The boys walked so fast that within three days, they caught up with the company. The officer Riel served, sent the two boys ahead to his home. One of his wives was to meet him on the way between Gogrial and Twic. Riel could proceed to visit his family a little further away to the east of the officer's home.

Riel was very happy to go and visit his family. Twic was one of the areas most devastated by the Arab militia, the Murahliin and the Nuer. However, the people still resolutely stayed and lived there.

3

The officer gave each of the boys an AK47 rifle with about three magazines. But each of them had other magazines hidden in their bags. The boys took their sleeping bags only. The officer's wife was to be accompanied by a runner the officer left in charge of his family. Riel and his friend Kedit were to proceed to Riel's home.

The two boys received a pass and went ahead of the company. The pass was to be presented to any SPLM man in charge of the area they passed through, to provide them with any necessary assistance, including food and not to tamper with their guns. The document did not state whether the two were soldiers or not.

When they arrived at the first SPLM camp, they presented their pass. They also asked for something to eat. But the officer in charge told the two that they were two days now without food to eat. "There is hunger in the area. It takes several days before we are able to get some food to eat," he said. The two could proceed ahead to other villages. Two persons can easily be fed by the local people.

While they were talking, a long line of wild ducks was approaching above the camp. The wild ducks flew in a line or two, all following each other. The long line was within range of the AK47. Other lines were flying some distance away. All were headed for the Toc, a few kilometers away.

Kedit requested the officer to allow them to kill the flying wild ducks, using their rifles. The officer laughed. "How can you kill flying ducks?" asked the officer.

"Allow us to fire at them," put in Kedit.

By the time the first ducks were over the camp, the officer said, "You can fire if you think you can kill any of them."

The two boys started to fire at the ducks. Before the birds could realize what was happening, a dozen or more of them came down dead, either in the middle of the camp or at its periphery.

The officer could not believe his eyes. Each of the boys killed as many as his gun could. Abdun killed more. The soldiers who were present or outside the camp compound came running to the scene. They were as stunned as their officer.

When the scene cleared it was found that most of the ducks were shot at the head and the neck. A few had wounds in the body or a broken wing.

That evening the soldiers feasted on bird meat. All had enough to eat. It was the first time in many days that they had enough delicious meat to eat. The following morning, the officer issued the boys with a new permit. To the officer, the two were SPLA soldiers. Although underage, they could be absorbed into the rank and file of the SPLA soldiers. The two did a wonderful job by rescuing their comrades from hunger.

The boys were happy. They pocketed the recommendation paper and left.

Arriving at the officer's home they were very well received. They delivered the message and on the following day the runner and two wives of the officer left.

They were to meet the officer in one of the villages along the road between Gogrial and Twic. The boys also departed to Riel's village about ten to fifteen miles away to the east.

Riel and his friend Kedit could not reach home. On the way, they stumbled upon a long line of SPLA soldiers, moving to Kiirkou. The Murahliin were reported to have come to attack the area. Without being asked, the two joined the soldiers and went along with them to Kiirkou, where the Murahliin were expected to launch an attack.

On the way they informed the commanding officer that the two of them had joined the force of their own accord. They thought, "We should be allowed to stick together. The soldiers in the force do not know us and we on the other hand, know no soldiers."

The commanding officer agreed and told them to be very careful. "The Murahliin are great fighters. You two must try to help each other in case of danger."

The boys were very happy. At last they were to experience their first combat. They congratulated each other and said to one another, "Let us see who is going to be the most courageous."

The following day they were attacked. The Murahliin came on horses and on foot. The small SPLA contingent was overwhelmed and scattered towards the evening hours. The two boys escaped into a small forest, which they thought was large enough. Behind the forest was a small, deserted village with a few scattered huts, many of them on poles. (The Dinka call them 'hot nhial' meaning *upper house*.)

Moving from one bush or shrub to another, the two emerged into the village. There was an open space between the boys and the huts on poles. Nothing could save them, except to run fast, and to go under one of the huts.

The two ran to a house which was isolated and near a stream. The hut stood some distance away from the rest of the houses. The stream made a curve almost around the hut, so much that anyone approaching it, had only one way to pass through.

The stream was full of water. The boys ran very fast to that hut. Three or four horses came galloping behind them. As soon as the boys were under the hut, the Murahliin stopped. They went back to where some of their fellow men stood.

The Murahliin stood in a group and seemed to be talking. After that, four horses, each carrying two persons or more, started to run at full speed, heading towards the hut. Kedit and Riel divided the horses among themselves. One was to shoot down two, and in no time, four horses with their riders were either dead or dying. All the riders were thrown off by the horses and fell head long.

The dying horses made a lot of dust. Abdun could not wait to see, what they had done. He threw away his gun and ran fast to where the Murahliin's rifles fell. He collected four from the two horses he had killed.

He ran back with them and threw them under the hut. Riel wanted to go and bring the guns of the other two riders he had killed, but Kedit shouted to him not to emerge, but to cover his movements. Other horses were coming to where their comrades had fallen.

Abdun again raced back with the speed of wind. He again collected the four rifles of the other two horses killed by Riel and ran back. As he threw the rifles again under the hut, Riel emerged and began to fire at the approaching horses. The riders turned and ran back before Riel was able to hit any of them.

When the boys saw that the riders went back, the two went and took all the magazines and bags carried by the fallen Murahliin. With that daring act, the two collected eight new AK47 rifles with several magazines filled with rounds of ammunitions. The two congratulated themselves and said to one another, "Now we can keep a company at bay. Let the Murahliin come back again."

The boys examined every rifle and found them intact and worth putting to use.

The Murahliin did not come back. Nature came to the aid of the boys. The sun was setting. By late evening, the two boys carried four rifles each with several magazines full of ammunition. They started to search for SPLA soldiers. They knew that no one would be found in the place besides soldiers.

Before eight o'clock, or after it, the two were found by a team of soldiers sent to search for them. No soldier saw any of the two being shot. The SPLA soldiers were very happy to find them alive and sound. Each of them was heavily weighed down by the load of guns and ammunition.

The Murahliin had been beaten back and returned to their home bases. The two boys proceeded to Riel's home. There at home, the boys always went fishing.

Riel's home was by the Toc and the people there fished in the rivers and ponds.

Abdun Kedit taught himself how to fish using a net and hooks. Before he came to this area, Kedit was not able to stand up straight or erect in a canoe with a fishing net in his arm ready to throw it into the water to catch fish. After two months the officers they served, ordered them back.

The two arrived in Aweil area. The area was to the far west of the railway line.

When the two arrived they presented two recommendations from two different officers. The officers they served were surprised at the recommendations. Their case was referred to the commanding officer of the battalion.

Two separate investigations were carried out. The boys were separated and investigated thoroughly. The recommendations were found genuine. What each told the investigators agreed word for word.

The officers, who made the recommendations, were also consulted and each confirmed the authenticity of what he had written. As the two were now over 18 years of age, it was recommended that they should be absorbed into the army and were also recommended for promotion to the rank of lieutenants.

CHAPTER TWO

I t was almost the end of April or early May, when Riel was assigned to a newly regrouped number of soldiers, who were either on leave or had left their units for various reasons. It was learned that the enemy was preparing an attack, although peace talks had progressed beyond expectations. The ceasefire had been holding for a long time. While the enemy talked with the movement, other opposition groups were not prepared to see peace achieved.

Military intelligence had intercepted an enemy message, requesting Sudan government units in the South to mount an attack on SPLA bases, a day before the peace agreement was to be signed. Some Arab friends, sympathetic to the movement also sent verbal messages to that effect. "Let all your units be at maximum alert seventy-two hours before the peace deal is to be signed and after it. If no attack is launched, then you can scale down but remain on the lookout."

It was for this reason that the unit was formed from various battalions and units. The soldiers were rounded up and drilled into an effective fighting unit. The soldiers in the unit did not know each other before, especially the elderly men.

A very young officer at the rank of 2nd lieutenant was to command the unit. The young officer was small in every sense of the word; small by birth, small in body and appeared as if he had never been in combat.

At the end of every training session, the elderly soldiers, most of them veterans of Anya-nya One and non-commissioned officers, joked and jeered at the young officer. They usually asked him, "How did you become commissioned to the rank of 2nd Lieutenant, young as you are? Who really recommended you to the Chairman? Are you related to the person who gave the recommendation or did you bribe that officer?

"When the enemy comes you will run away as a child which you are. You have never seen the stain of blood in a battlefield. Many of us here have been in many dangerous combats since Anya-nya One.

"Several of our comrades remained behind on the battlefield dead, wounded or captured by the enemy. You will not withstand the enemy's intensive gunfire, the blood and lamentation of those wounded and rolling with pain near you."

The young Lieutenant was also a jolly person. He did not take their taunting remarks to heart. He told them, "You are not aware how I have been under heavy fire before. Once there is an attack you can count on me. I am young but I am as brave as a buffalo. I can fight like a lion. Only one person, a friend of mine, younger than myself knows about me. When we are together we are like devils in any combat.

"I miss his company very much. He is an Agar from Rumbek, named Kedit. Although small in every sense of the word, as you say, his father gave him an exact name, Kedit — *yen ee kedit alanden*, in anything he does. The two of us can enter Hell and still extricate ourselves from the Devil in his abode, let alone come out of a combat. Kedit is very brave, a great marksman, as I am, but faster in movement and running.

"I got this AK47 which I carry from the Arab Murahliin. Kedit has another. Both are Iraqi made. Who among you here carries one? It is said an Iraqi AK47 is the best in the battlefield. The Iraqi made AK47 is not commonly found with SPLA soldiers. I know of a few which Kedit and myself captured in the forests between Aweil and Raga.

"What took place in those areas and how we got commissioned will be a story once the peace agreement is signed. Or I may relate it, once the expected imminent attack is beaten off and we come back safe and sound. When that happens you will not doubt my capability and leadership to lead you into battle and back again alive."

For more than two months Riel had been training with the regrouped old soldiers. He was ready to do anything for the old Anya-nya One combatants. Although Riel was an officer he offered his services to his elderly non-commissioned officers. It is never expected that an officer serves non-commissioned officers and soldiers. He made tea for them and at times brought them water, especially after hard and difficult training in the scorching hot sun. The elderly soldiers became easily tired and exhausted. They were not able to move or help themselves.

Riel the lieutenant was always available to render services to his old soldiers. Almost all the elderly soldiers loved the young man. But still they regarded him as a boy. The men encouraged Riel every time he served them. They asked the Creator to pour his blessings upon the young man, to survive the war and to progress to the highest position after the war.

CHAPTER THREE

When no attack came and the peace deal had been signed, Riel one morning told his elderly non-commissioned officers, "After seventy-two hours I will relate to you the things I did. First, how I got enlisted into the army, secondly and thirdly how I was recognized to become a soldier and then how I got commissioned. All these did not take many years. I was a regular soldier for about five or six years and an officer within this short period.

"I am not a relative of the officer or officers who recommended my friend Kedit and me. As young men we have no wealth or anything like that to bribe a senior officer to recommend us to the Chairman and Commander in Chief of the SPLA. The ranks were awarded to us through hard fighting with the enemy. The fights we carried out were recognized and we were rewarded by our senior officers who were impressed with our war efforts and combat."

Seventy-two hours after the peace agreement was signed and no attack was launched, Riel's unit was to be disbanded. The elderly non-commissioned officers were to go back to their former mother units. Riel was ordered to report to his former unit or company. Riel's company had gone back to Rumbek, their former base.

In the morning of the fourth day, Riel called the whole unit together. He first told them, "By the tenth day of peace all of us will have to go back to our former units if those are nearby. Those whose units are far will have to walk there to wait for further orders or the reorganization of the whole army during peace time. I myself will leave for Rumbek where my company is stationed.

"Today is going to be a special one. The commander has sent us that big fat bull you see tied under the tree. First go and kill it and roast some of the meat on the fire. We are to eat burnt meat under that big shady tree. There I am going to relate to you how I become a regular soldier, then an officer, while my age was between eighteen and twenty-three years. I do not want any of you to go away with a wrong impression about me — how I became a soldier and then gained the position of lieutenant. Many of you are of my father's age and that is why I render services to you."

Ayualdit, the most talkative elderly non-commissioned officer said, "Do not take the jokes we used to tell you to heart. We here are very happy that a person of your caliber was placed at the head of us. Our talk was to encourage you to gain the experience and skills a soldier needs and which I think you possess. You served us as if you were one of our children. You did not behave in a way officers normally do.

"We bless you in our hearts and in our prayers to the Creator. We all wish you success and advancement in the army. Now that peace has come, old people like me will have to retire and young soldiers like you will continue in the army.

"From today, know that our blessings will follow you to old age. *Nhialic abi doc* and takes care of you. I wish you to survive in peace. I once heard from an officer what a great Nigerian writer wrote. The officer told us that, 'It is one thing to survive in war and another to survive during peace time.' The Nigerian wrote a book titled, *How to Survive Peace*. That was after the Biafran war.

"Peace comes with its own problems. One must overcome those obstacles otherwise one may not survive it. Let me tell you now — be prepared to survive peace my son.

"Many of us are Anya-nya One veterans. Many of my age mates and comrades in arms did not survive the peace of those days. I survived it and I hope to survive the present coming one. You go and slaughter our bull. Let us eat and be merry. The good Lord has preserved us alive. We shall listen to the talk of our young lieutenant."

CHAPTER FOUR

Riel said: Kedit and I met in Rumbek. I served an officer from my area when I was a teenage boy. The school I was in got shut down suddenly when all our teachers were rounded up by the soldiers and marched to the front or to where the fighting was taking place. We could do nothing. Most of our teachers were trained as soldiers.

I had to serve a captain, who commanded a unit in my area, in order to get something to eat. There was famine in our area. As he comes from my area, he treated me nicely. I had enough to eat and free time to play.

Once my morning duties were over, I joined the soldiers in whatever they did. I ran with them any distance they covered. I practiced how to dismantle and put back all the parts of a gun as quickly as they did. I climbed obstacles and tall trees as demanded by the trainers.

I was not allowed to practice shooting when the soldiers did that. But I remained near them to see how the soldiers aimed and fired at the targets. The target a soldier missed, I thought I would not have missed. That's how my daily routine was spent.

Then my young officer was ordered to leave for Rumbek with his company. I left with him carrying his sleeping bags and other small accessories of an officer. By the time we arrived at Rumbek, the city had fallen to the SPLA. There was nothing for the soldiers, who were ordered to capture the city, to do. Some units were ordered to follow those who captured Rumbek to Tonj and other towns, which were still under the Sudan Government Army's control.

Captain Akuoc, whom I served, remained to keep peace and order in Rumbek town and its vicinity. He and captain Riak, from Rumbek, stayed in one of the captured houses. It was there that I found my friend Kedit. He was smaller than me in body build and age. He was also taller and thinner than me. He served captain Riak.

The circumstances which made him serve captain Riak were similar to mine. Rumbek town was besieged by the SPLA for several months before it fell. All the schools in and around Rumbek got closed. Some school children went home to their parents. Others like Kedit, who were interested in the army or in search of something to eat like myself came to serve the soldiers, not as combatants, but to render services in the military compounds.

As soon as I met Kedit we became great friends at once. His interests and mine were almost the same. We attended every military training and practiced with the soldiers. We covered several miles running with the soldiers. We went without a drink for more than twenty-four hours, when the soldiers were ordered not to take water or food. We practiced how to handle every gun available in Rumbek. A large number of guns, ammunition and other ordinances lay everywhere in the town, left behind by the defeated Sudan Government Army.

The two of us stealthily went and practiced on our own, with every gun we found lying about. We would not miss, even when we were told 'danger looms around them.'

We had light work to do in the house. Captain Riak's wife did most of the household duties. She would not allow us to clean the house, even the room of captain Akuoc. We could only help her, washing and ironing the clothes of the officers. When there was no washing, or cleaning and greasing the guns, we were as free as the birds. We ate and escaped to where most of the abandoned government army guns lay in great number.

The two of us always became easily bored. All that we performed was a repetition. We wanted something new and exciting. We learned a great deal about arms and how to use them. We wanted to practice firing at targets, but that was not allowed. We were prevented from doing so.

One day, Kedit heard that his father had fallen sick at

home. He told captain Riak that his father was seriously ill. He asked for permission to go and visit his sick father. Riak assented to his request. Kedit again went to captain Akuoc to allow me to accompany him to his home. Akuoc was very sympathetic, and he gave his consent, but Kedit should have asked me first, if I was willing and ready to go with him. Kedit knew that I would not turn him down. He told captain Akuoc that I would agree to accompany him, and so we went.

Before leaving Rumbek, we stole two new AK47 automatic rifles, with several magazines. Each of us carried a bag full of bullets. The bags were so heavy that it took us three days to arrive at Kedit's home, a distance of one day's walk.

To my surprise Kedit's home was near a river full of water throughout the year. After resting for two days, we began to practise swimming in the river. I knew how to swim, but not fast enough and not how to cross a river with a strong running current. After becoming tired, we started to practise firing at targets. Here, no one resented hearing the sound of gunshots. The chief and the elders of the area allowed us to practice. One time we killed a very huge hippo. The whole village feasted on its meat for several days. We killed several other small antelopes and wild pigs from time to time for the people in the village. At times the chief and the elders would ask us, to get an animal's meat for them.

We also practiced firing at the flying birds, especially

wild ducks, which were very common in the area. When the wild ducks became scared and no longer flew near the village, we turned to small doves. Each of us was to take off the dove's head without touching its body. In all these activities, each of us wanted to do better than the other in firing AK47's without missing the target.

We could not have anticipated the time or the number of months we spent in the village. Wildlife and fish were also in abundance. We fished and killed a wild animal when there was need for meat and for broth. Our time in the village went without our notice. Riak had to send his runner to call us back to Rumbek. We left the village forlornly. Our happy days seemed to have come to an end.

CHAPTER FIVE

Arriving in Rumbek, we found that the company had been ordered to move to Northern Bahr el Ghazal. By then Northern Bahr el Ghazal was comprised of Tonj, Gogrial and Aweil areas. We were to follow the company. Captain Riak's wife told us where we were to find the company.

We picked up the few things which were left for us to carry. This time, we had put on weight. We were fat to put it plainly. So, we carried those things left to us with ease. We loaded ourselves with more magazines full of ammunition. We also took with us the AK47 automatic rifles we had stolen before, when we left for Kedit's home.

The company left a week before our arrival in Rumbek. We had to walk hard and fast to join the force. We reached the force after three days. The officers we served were very glad to see us. Riak remarked, 'Boys, you are men by now.' Akuoc also said, 'What did you eat to become so fat like this?'

We were happy to hear their compliments about us. They did not ask us about the guns, nor did they tell us to give them up. Each of us wore an army uniform, which we also stole, when we went to the village, including boots and other army equipment. We appeared like any other soldier, even though the officers and men still regarded us as small boys or minors. I had turned eighteen and Kedit was seventeen.

Although we had put on weight, we still ran as fast as before and even more so. Kedit was still taller and leaner when I looked at him. I was some inches shorter, but no soldier could pass us in running, jumping, climbing obstacles and even target shooting, which we did not practise in the presence of the old soldiers. We told this to the soldiers who were our friends that we could outdo them in anything they did. They laughed and poo-pooed our remarks.

After spending a week with the company, Captain Akuoc asked the two of us to go and inform one of his wives to meet him on the road between Gogrial and Twic. He gave us the woman's name. She was to come with one of his runners. He also named the runner. As for us, we were to proceed to my home. We should remain there for not more than a month. He gave us a pass, known by then as a 'camp pass.'

The pass did not indicate whether we were soldiers or not, but any SPLA officer we found should render assistance to us, and also not tamper with our guns. It read, 'Captain Akuoc is sending these two young men to his home in Twic.'

We did not take a straight path to the officer's home. We decided to walk toward the Toc area between Apuok and Twic. We would come around later. I knew where we would find the SPLA camp, and where Twic cattle camps yearly spend the dry season. It was now the beginning of early rains and wild ducks were in their thousands in the Toc.

'Let us first go and kill as many wild ducks, as possible', I told Kedit. I also told Kedit how large the wild duck population was in that area Toc. At times they flew over the area at very close range and in long lines end to end, every morning and evening. There are several places in Twic and Apuok where the birds' movement is always in search of food, especially at the beginning of the rains. I said, 'We can practise killing them while flying.'

The first camp we found was almost deserted. Many soldiers had taken French leave. There was no food to come by. Most of the cattle camps had moved further away from where the SPLA camp was established. The soldiers here went for several days without food or milk. We found a few miserable soldiers in and around the camp to guard the heavy guns. They lay under the trees without expecting any food, but they were duty bound to guard the guns hungry or not.

We presented our camp pass, as it was known. The officer said, 'You can spend the night here and see for yourself whether we can eat anything. There is nothing eatable in this village. Many of my soldiers have gone to nearby villages to search for something to eat. The nearest cattle camps are more than six miles from here. The soldiers sent there this morning may come back tonight or not, depending on what they find.'

We went and sat alone in the shade of a hut. There were no seats or stools. The time was between 5:30-6:30 in the evening. Looking westward, I saw several lines of wild ducks flying to the Toc east of us. Every evening the wild ducks flew in either direction to the east or to the west. I told Kedit to look at the long lines of several thousands of wild ducks approaching over the compound. Kedit rushed to the officer and asked him to allow us to kill the ducks flying over the camp.

The officer was hesitant. First, he was afraid that firing a gun might frighten the villages around. Second, he was not sure whether we could shoot accurately at flying objects. Kedit assured him, that we could. Our man gave his consent.

Kedit signaled to me and within a few seconds or minutes, two to three dozen wild ducks covered the camp compound dead or dying. Many of them were shot in the head and the neck. A few were shot in the body. Kedit downed more ducks than me. That evening and the following day, the soldiers had enough birds' meat to eat.

The officer was surprised at our skillful shooting. He had never witnessed such accurate firing before. When he enquired about our positions in the army, we informed him that we were not conscripted into the army. We were still regarded as minors, although one of us was over eighteen years old.

Before we left, the officer commended all of us highly to be conscripted into the army, and if it was done, to be promoted to the rank of non-commissioned officers. He related in detail what we did to save his soldiers from dying of hunger. That was the first recommendation rendered to us.

CHAPTER SIX

Our other commendation came about the following way. Leaving the house of Captain Akuoc on our way to my home we met an SPLA force marching to Kiirkou. The soldiers were to reinforce a company stationed there. It was reported that the Murahliin were launching an attack. They were already in Abiei area, where they usually receive food, ammunition, additional horses and soldiers. The attack was to take place within two days.

We decided to join the force by volunteering for combat. We asked the commanding officer to allow us to go with them. No officer in his right mind would reject a soldier volunteering to go and fight. The officer did not ask where we came from or from which unit and company. He was happy that two more soldiers of their own accord had increased the number of his men.

The officer said to us, 'The Murahliin are great fighters. You must be careful when the fighting commences.' He also told us that he did not have enough bullets, in fact none to spare for us. Most of his soldiers had either one or two magazines at most.

We told him that we were prepared. We had two or more magazines each. He should not mind about us as far as the means to fight with is concerned. All that we requested from him was to allow the two of us to stick together. We did not know his soldiers, and they on the other hand did not know how we fight.

It was a lie. We had not been in combat before. But the officer agreed. He instructed one of his senior non-commissioned officers to let us remain close to each other. He should also come to our support when need arose.

The NCO instructed the two of us to be very careful. 'Don't allow the Murahliin on horseback to get behind you. The horsemen are the ones who always broke through our lines. A horse carries two to three soldiers. Two of them jump off the horse. It is those left behind who begin to attack and kill the soldiers from behind. Then there, they create a gap in the lines of our fighters.

'Make sure, no horseman or horsemen go behind you. Also be economical with your rounds. No one will give you extra bullets. Also observe the movement of our soldiers. When a break is made by the enemy in our lines or our ammunition runs low, the soldiers will begin to escape one by one from the battlefield.

'See to it that you are not left behind, in case we are overwhelmed. I will give you a special signal, to move out or run, but move in an orderly fashion. Shoot at the horses, not at the riders. Once a horse is hit, it throws off the rider or riders. In most cases, the riders are instantly killed. If any are left alive, they will be out of action.'

We treasured the NCO's talks. At night we repeated to each other all that the man told us. We also decided to fight along the edge of the battle line near a small stream. The stream contained water. The Arabs are of short stature and most of them do not swim. The Baggara Arabs, who make up the bulk of the Murahliin do not swim, as they have no rivers to practise the art. If we prevent them from getting around us to the rear, they will not be able to break through on our wing.

In the morning, the Arabs attacked us. We mowed down every horse or foot soldier who came along the stream. They had to avoid where we were. We fought for more than five hours, then there was a lull toward midday. Our man the NCO came up to us crawling. He congratulated us highly. 'Keep to it like that,' he said. 'Keep on that way my boys,' he told us a second time. 'Check your rounds. The horsemen will come in a wave, maybe without the foot soldiers. They have realized that it has been difficult to break through with a few horses. All of them are going to attack in great numbers soon or in the late afternoon.'

Before, the NCO had finished talking, we saw a group of horsemen assembling and pointing in our direction. This time we replaced our magazines. Each of us fixed in the gun a magazine which contained tracer bullets. We had filled two magazines each with only tracer bullets.

We reasoned that tracer rounds would be deadly to horses even if a horse was not fatally hit. Our idea worked. Several horses raced towards us in order to break through. As we were sharp shooters, we brought down all the horses which came in our direction. The other horses had to turn aside. Before three o'clock our lines broke. Most of our soldiers ran low on ammunition. Some of them had less than five rounds left. The NCO signaled to us to pull back into the bushes which were behind us. We thought a forest was behind into which we could escape.

We saw a group of soldiers running away from the enemy. Many of them were hit and they fell down dead or dying. Those who avoided the enemy's bullets ran under a few huts on poles, the Dinka people call *hot nhial*. Once under those huts, the pursuers stopped and turned back to chase the other soldiers who were still running.

When the horsemen saw the two of us escaping, they turned in our direction. There was one isolated hut on poles about half a kilometer away. We raced towards it at top speed. The horsemen thought they could overtake us. The riders were not able to shoot at us while their horses were running. They could not overtake us because each horse carried three men. A rider could not jump off a horse while it was running fast, and if they slowed down to allow a rider to jump off, we would escape from them. We were only two and they were sure to get us, no matter what happened or how fast we ran.

We ran faster than the horsemen anticipated. We entered under the hut and from there, we turned around and shot down the first four horses and twelve riders fell dead or dying. Twelve or more guns fell with them.

Kedit, seeing the horses and the riders on the ground and making a cloud of dust around them, ran back at once. He picked up four guns lying near the dead soldiers. I wanted to do the same, but he shouted to me not to come out but to cover his movements. Some horses were coming to the rescue of their fallen comrades, or to collect their guns and kill us, if that were possible.

Kedit threw the four guns under the hut and we both ran to the two other fallen horses. Seeing me rushing towards them, the horsemen beat a hasty retreat until they were outside the range of my gun. Kedit took the other four guns. He returned a fourth time and picked up the magazines stashed on the dead Murahliin. Each dead Marhal carried several magazines.

After Kedit had gathered every magazine from the fallen enemy we went under the hut and rested for a while. We were still alert and surveyed the country in every direction around us. The horsemen, several in number, stood about half a kilometer away. They appeared to be talking or planning what to do next.

Kedit examined all the guns we had captured. All were brand new and in good working condition and were Iraqi made. It was said in SPLA circles that AK47's made in Iraq were the best on the battlefield. Now *we* had them. Kedit selected one for himself and handed another to me.

By now we had enough ammunition to keep a company at bay. We arranged and placed the magazines in such a way that we could easily pick them up one by one when the other was spent. It was under the hut on poles that we began to feel thirsty and somewhat hungry.

We were alone. We did not know what had happened to the rest of our comrades. The sun was setting, and the enemy did not come back. The place became very quiet, quiet as a graveyard. There was no wind, no sound anywhere or movement by anybody. The two of us, could not even talk. It was our first battle. The dead Murahliin and the horses lay sinister in front of us.

It was the first time either of us had killed a human being. We began to shiver and be afraid. We had no idea what to do next. Was that the end of the fight or would there be another attack? Our comrades and even the enemy were nowhere near. We did not know what to do or how we would carry all the captured guns and ammunition.

CHAPTER SEVEN

The moon rose around eight o'clock and we heard the voices of a group of people talking and moving somewhere near us. We heard their talk. We talked aloud in order to let them know that there were people near the hut. They responded and called back to us.

The people turned out to be soldiers. They came straight to us. 'Don't shoot at us, we are looking for you,' remarked the senior NCO, who was assigned to help and protect us. We recognized his voice. We called out to him, 'Sergeant major Amou, we are here!' Sergeant major Amou responded very heartily, 'Are you there my boys?'

'Yes,' we replied.

The soldiers all rushed to us. They were very happy to find us.

'We came to search for you, my boys,' said sergeant major Amou. 'You did wonders to the enemy. We thought the enemy would break through on your side. But neither those on horseback nor those on foot did. Young men come with us.'

Kedit told the sergeant major that we had captured some guns and ammunition. 'Let the soldiers help us to carry them.' The soldiers all rushed forwards at once, and said, 'Where are they?'

'Go under the hut and you will find them,' said Kedit.

One soldier bent down under the hut. 'My dear!' he shouted. 'There are many guns, pouches and bags containing bullets, and magazines also filled with bullets.' He started to ferry them out one by one. Ready hands were waiting to catch and carry them.

The soldiers were all surprised. It was one of those rare instances when several Murahliin guns got captured by the SPLA soldiers, but the enemy had actually pushed us back and got us running for dear life. Our forces were dramatically driven away with the loss of several soldiers. According to the soldiers, they did not expect to find us alive. It was the sergeant major who insisted that they search for us. He had seen us rush under the hut.

Sergeant major Amou wanted to make sure whether the two of us were alive or dead. Fighting had been intense on our side before the enemy broke through the ranks of our forces. But the forces on our side withdrew in order under the huts. The enemy turned and chased the soldiers who took to their heels. Many of those soldiers were now dead.

We all marched back to the main camp. In the morning, the commanding officer of the company gave orders to go back to make a search of the previous day's battle ground. Early morning reports indicated that the enemy had withdrawn. We should go and bury the corpses of our dead comrades, if that were possible, especially the officers who had lost their lives.

Many of the soldiers selected declined to go. Most of them gave lame excuses for not going. The two of us decided to volunteer again and joined those who were ready to go. No one objected. Those going hailed our decision.

On the way, we were told by the soldiers to be very careful and attentive. 'Soldiers inspecting a battlefield are often killed by the wounded left behind. Our own wounded soldiers might even kill us because we left them to the mercy of the enemy. If the enemy had found them, they could have been finished off. The wounded do not differentiate between a friend and a foe.

'As for the enemy soldiers, it is what they do best. They know that their lives will not be spared. They have to get rid of searchers before they themselves are finished off. You boys, when you see a prone body, don't assume it to be of a dead soldier. Be cautious. Put yourself in a position that he cannot directly fire at you.

'When you suspect or see a body to be that of a soldier still alive, get rid of it if it is that of an enemy. If it is one of our comrades, approach him in such a way that he cannot easily or quickly turn to fire at you. The wounded soldiers also hide in the grass, under the trees and in the bushes. They can easily kill you before you are aware of their presence there.

We spent the whole day, searching on our side and that of the enemy. Many dead bodies we found were of our comrades. The enemy had either carried away the corpses of their dead, dumped them in the stream or buried them along the stream which was soft and easy for burial. We found a few enemy soldiers wounded. They hid themselves in some bushes. We had no alternative but to finish them off.

At night we could not sleep well. Wild dreams, of the dead and dying hounded us, especially me. The person who slept near us had to wake us now and then, because of the shouts each of us uttered. To be honest, it was the first time for the two of us, to witness such mass death. Corpses lay everywhere we went. Flies and swarms of other insects covered the dead bodies. Even bees landed in the blood of the dead and sucked at it. Now I hate eating honey.

In the morning of the following day, the commander of the company summoned the two of us to his office. He congratulated us profusely and very warmly. He ordered us to leave the camp at once, and head off. He wrote a very elaborate recommendation for us. He said, 'Take this to your commander.'

CHAPTER EIGHT

Two days later, we found ourselves at my home, though it could not be called a home. Most of the houses had been torched and reduced to ashes by the Arabs. My father had erected a few small huts of twigs and grass. They were covered with plastic sheets to keep out the rain. During the heat of the day, it was as hot as hell. There were no cows nor other domestic animals. All the citizens in the area lived on fish and some food supplied by the World Food Program and other NGO's.

After staying a month, we were ordered to leave for the Aweil area. The officers we served had been ordered to move to the far west of the railway line. Their company was to reinforce the troops in that area. The area was like Twic. It had been drastically destroyed year after year.

Some friendly Arabs come to graze their cattle in the area. They had signed a memorandum of understanding with the movement. But at times they provoked a fight with the SPLA when returning to Darfur at the beginning of the rainy season. Before the end of the rains, their elders and chiefs come again to apologize for what their youth had done and to pay compensation for whatever losses were caused, especially the human ones.

The movement benefited from those friendly Arab tribes, financially and materially. The Arabs brought with them food items and other merchandise. They paid taxes to the movement which allowed them to graze their cattle.

During their stay, grazing their cattle, they become very friendly, meek and obedient. They brought a lot of goods into the area which were not available in most of the SPLA controlled areas. People from other areas such as Gogrial up to Tonj and sometimes Rumbek, came to the area to buy most of their essential supplies, such as soap, sugar, salt and clothes.

Trading in cattle was also encouraged. Arabs from elsewhere went there to buy cattle. The bulls and oxen were driven to cattle markets in Darfur, Kordofan and even up to Khartoum at the beginning of the rainy season. Money in the form of cash also became available, which would not have been there if trade in cattle had not been facilitated.

We left my home after a month's stay. We did not enjoy life in the area. Wildlife was available in great number, but we were not allowed to fire a gun even at wild ducks. It was strictly prohibited to fire a gun. The sound of a single gunshot signified that the enemy had come to attack and the population must run away or escape to safe places, beyond the enemy's reach.

We left the area hurriedly with the runner sent to take us to the officers we served. The distance involved meant it took us about four days, at a fast walk. Upon our arrival, we presented the two letters of recommendation. The letter of the last officer who had led us into battle, amazed every officer who read it.

The two letters of recommendation were passed to the commanding officer of the area. He ordered us to be brought before him on the fourth day of our arrival. All that he said was, 'From now on you are SPLA soldiers.' We were then assigned to a platoon. The platoon commander also assigned us to a unit, which he told us was the best. The soldiers in the unit were the bravest and the best fighters. We would fit into their ranks without difficulty.

Later, we learnt that those who gave us recommendations stated that we should be allowed to remain together. Our Iraqi made AK47's were to be left to us. They were the only Iraqi made guns in the whole battalion. Every officer had his eye on them. But the commander requested all the officers who were to command us not to tamper with them. 'The guns were captured by force. Anyone wanting an Iraqi made AK47 submachine gun should get one in the same way the young men got theirs,' they said. Every officer or soldier, who saw us carrying these guns envied us. Some soldiers were bold enough to enquire, 'How did you come by those guns?' None of them believed our story, especially the way Abdun ran to take the guns while the enemy was rushing at us.

We told the skeptical that a horse rider could not kill a person while his horse was still running. It is only when the rider jumps off his horse that he is able to shoot at a target. We gave the riders no opportunity to dismount from their horses. All fell at once, horse and rider before they were able to take position and aim. There was some distance between the first four horses we brought down and those which followed them. Seeing four horses down, the other horse riders turned back. Their turning back gave Kedit a chance to collect all the guns, pouches, bags and magazines.

The other riders retired about a kilometer away to confer with each other and other riders. The Murahliin did not come back. Only the two of us remained under the hut till the sun went down. The sight of the dead was very frightening. It was the first time we witnessed death through killing with a gun.

Thus, Riel ended his speech to the Anya-nya One veterans.

CHAPTER NINE

One afternoon towards the end of April or early May a year later, three horsemen rode to the headquarters of the SPLA commander of the area. The commander and most of his senior officers were playing cards. It was a very hot Sunday noon. Almost everybody sat to the east of every hut or tree, all in the shade to avoid the intense heat.

Sunday was usually a rest day when no news of an attack was reported. This is why many officers gathered to play cards. The SPLA military area was a very large one, with lots and lots of grass huts erected, for officers' and men's lodgings and training grounds.

The commanders' huts and a large officers' mess stood in the middle of the compound. Most senior officers played that day with the commander. Playing cards of whist started right after breakfast, till the Arab horsemen arrived. The junior officers played also in another part or remained sitting idle where their units were accommodated.

The Arab horsemen would not dismount from their horses. They called the commander by name and whispered to him in low voices. They rode off at once, as soon as they had delivered their message.

The commander went back to the officers and threw down the cards he held in his hands. All the senior officers rose to listen to what the commander had to say. The commander reported to the listeners the Arabs' mission.

After delivering what he heard from the Arabs, the commander ordered his deputy to blow his whistle. A trumpet was also sounded. It was for an emergency, and it was blown. All the senior officers were ordered to move to their headquarters at once and wait for orders to move out of the military area to new positions. In less than an hour orders were issued to every fighting unit to move to new positions along the river, and to proceed until they found a place where the river was full of water. The soldiers should not go further after finding a location where the river contained enough water to prevent the Arabs from crossing. (The Arabs are short people and almost all of them do not swim.)

The message brought by the three Arab horsemen was that the government of Sudan had amassed a very large force composed of the army and the militia to accompany the trains heading to Wau. Between two and three thousand horsemen were assembled along river Kiir from south-western Kordofan up to the far eastern Darfur. Over two thousand horsemen were to attack and sweep away SPLA forces up to a distance of fifteen to twenty miles on both sides of the railway.

Another thousand soldiers and militiamen on foot were assigned east of and west of the railway line, along its length. No village or people, cattle or any living thing were to be left on either side of the rail line. The militias were to take whatever loot was found on their way as booty; people or cattle plus arms captured from the SPLA forces. The government had no need of prisoners of war, or any booty captured.

Women, girls and children captured were to be owned by those who took them captives. The militiamen were free to commit any crime. No power in this country or anywhere could restrain them or question their actions. The militiamen were fighting on behalf of Allah and the nation. The Almighty would absolve them from killing kufar or infidels.

The three horsemen, who brought the message were from the friendly Arabs of Darfur. Those friendly Arab tribes come to SPLA controlled areas every year to graze their cattle. These Arab nomads helped the movement by bringing food items and other merchandisable goods to the area, besides providing the information needed about the government's intentions. They also told their people how to conduct themselves when the attackers arrived.

When those friendly Arab tribes arrive in the South, they leave all their arms and ammunition at the headquarters of the SPLA forces they come in contact with at the border. A few guns are left to them in order to protect their cattle and maybe themselves from wild animals. They are allowed to graze up to the road between Wau and Raja. They are told not to kill wild animals. They could fish and search for honey in the forests where their cattle graze.

The friendly Arab tribes adhered to these arrangements for several years. The three men came to inform the movement about the eminent attack. They feared the large militia forces would overwhelm the forces of the movement or the forces at the front. They were also afraid that the arms of their people which were in the custody of the SPLA could be taken by the attacking militia forces. That act would deprive their people of the means of defending themselves and their cattle upon their return home. If they went back without their guns, the tribes friendly to the Sudan Government would provoke a fight, in order to kill them and take their cattle.

'The Sudan Government has allowed the tribes friendly to them to take our cattle. The government would not bother to listen to us in the case of our wealth being looted.'

The horsemen's next move was to inform their people with the cattle to be on the alert. They asked the commander to allow the friendly Arabs in the forests of South Sudan to take their arms from the SPLA stores, so that they could defend themselves and their animals. If the request was turned down, they would go and tell their people to move back deep into the forests, where the militiamen would not be able to reach them.

Most of their cattle camps were returning to the river site because of early rains which had started to fall. They did not want their cattle to remain south of the river during the rainy season. Once the river is full of water, they would be cut off. The horsemen wanted their people to cross the river while the water in the river was a foot high.

The commander refused to allow the guns to be taken. He told the three men that the SPLA was going to protect their arms and cattle.

'We shall beat off the attack,' the commander informed the three men. 'Go and tell your people to move back into the forests till the attack is beaten off. Your guns are in safe hands. If the river becomes full, we shall help you cross the river as our people do when going north while the river is full, up to the maximum.'

After informing the senior officers, the commander allowed each officer to move to new positions. Platoon number one, in which Kedit and Riel were assigned, was ordered to walk as quickly as possible to where the river water had accumulated and was full. They were to stop there and guard it till they were ordered back. The attack was expected to take place within seventy-two hours, starting from six o'clock the next morning.

The militiamen were assigned to cross anywhere along

the river. Their intention was to make a flank attack at SPLA positions and from the front. The arrangement was to cordon off the SPLA on all sides, and then eliminate them, thus clearing the movement away from the railway line on both sides, west and east up to Aweil and Wau.

The SPLA headquarters informed by the horsemen was on the western side of the railway covering most of east and western Darfur. The troops here had to move further westward up to where the river contained enough water to prevent the militia attackers from crossing to the south of the river. The three horsemen told the SPLA commander of the area that the militias were already moving to the river on horseback.

The trains were reported to have left Muglad seventy-two hours previously. They would stop at Bahr el Arab railway station waiting for the militia attack. The trains were bringing essential supplies, arms and ammunition to Bahr el Ghazal military area for the rainy season. No more trains would be coming till the next dry season in November or December.

The commander of the platoon on the western side, which Kedit and Riel belonged to, ordered his men to move out at once. The soldiers assembled, took up their weapons and other war and personal equipment and left. The company walked for several hours nonstop till the early morning hours of the following day. A very heavy rain fell while the soldiers were moving. A lot of lightning and thunder was seen and heard all over the area. It appeared as if the gods were angry and were fighting each other. Lightning strike after lightning strike illuminated the sky throughout the night, and red lights glowed in the sky.

By morning most of their personal belongings and equipment were soaked. The officers of the units ordered the soldiers to continue moving, even if all their things were wet. It is a heavy burden to carry soaked things, plus arms and ammunitions. Fatigue and hunger began to bite at the soldiers.

However, orders were to be obeyed. The soldiers were there to protect themselves and their country people. They would stop only where the river contained enough water to prevent the militiamen from crossing.

After walking for some morning hours, the soldiers saw a pool in the middle of the river, full of water. The first soldiers to see it were Kedit and Riel. They marched ahead of their unit every time the platoon was on the move.

Kedit and Riel stopped and told their commanding officer that they had seen water in a pool in the river. The officer ordered the two of them to go and ascertain whether it was a stagnant isolated pool containing water during the dry season.

Returning, they reported that water was flowing into the pool from the far west. The pool was a deep one and must get full first before the water begins to flow out of it to the east.

The officer ordered the soldiers to pull back and stop

under some shady trees to rest and to dry most of their personal belongings which were still wet. It was already midday, and the sun was hot. The soldiers pulled back about two to the three hundred meters from the river and about half a kilometer from the pool of water.

CHAPTER TEN

A few shrubs were here and there between the river and where the soldiers settled in under the trees. The soldiers started at once to spread out all that was wet to dry. Some of them settled down and took a nap. Others cleaned and greased their guns. Kedit and Riel sat alone, some distance away from the rest of their comrades. They talked about the impending attack, and how they were going to inflict causalities on the enemy and save the lives of their comrades and people.

The two agreed to stick together as before. 'Let what may come, come.' They took a nap for about an hour. When they woke, the time was between four thirty and five thirty in the evening. Kedit picked up his gun with one magazine only, and Riel did the same. But he had an extra magazine, strapped to his gun. They decided to go to the riverbank, near the pool full of water. They were thinking they might take a bath in the fresh water of early rains. They left all their things where they took a nap. Their clothes remained spread on the shrubs to dry in the sun.

The two young men had not walked far when they saw a horse jump out of the river and another and another and another. The two ran to the scene. They could not watch to ascertain what was taking place. Both fired at once at the horse, which was trying to run after the other horses and the one which was emerging from the river.

The horse was hit and it went back rolling into the river with its rider. Both horseman and the two young men were surprised to see each other. Kedit and Riel went behind a small bush and when a horse emerged, they fired at it and it went back again rolling. A horse which had previously come out of the river went back behind the bushes. The young men saw it and fired at it. The horse and its rider fell down dead.

Kedit at once repeated what he did in the previous fight against the Murahliin. He rushed out to get hold of the gun. A militia man, hidden, shot at him. He was missed very narrowly, but the gun he held was smashed into fragments. Riel shouted to him to come back to where he was. He immediately knocked off the man's head.

Riel shot two more horses which were coming to the scene of the action. Other horses raced to where the gun shots were coming from. Kedit ran to where Riel was without a gun. The two depended only on one gun. Many horsemen emerged from the river. The two had to escape for dear life. They were cut off from the rest of their forces.

More and more horsemen emerged and went after the two young men. Riel shot down several horses while his magazine contained some bullets. He was running low on ammunition when he fixed the last magazine into the gun. The few rounds left would not have lasted long had the sun not gone down.

The two ran from bush to bush, till darkness covered the forest. The militia men could not see them. They settled quietly under a small shrub and remained there concealed. Several horsemen passed a few meters away from their hiding place at a gallop hunting for them, but the young men were not visible to the searchers.

The militia horsemen called off their search for the young men. They went back to where fighting was still raging. The two young men could hear gun shots, east of where they were. When the fighting died down or when they could not hear the sound of guns, they left the bush, but they did not know where to move to.

The two had only one gun with a few rounds left. The forest was becoming thick, dense and dark. They walked a few kilometers to the west. The grass here had grown to about a meter high. Heavy clouds had gathered and covered the sky and rain was imminent. The young men decided to walk southward far from the theatre of combat.

After a day or two, they would turn eastward, expecting

the militia to have left the area, or to have been beaten back. The Arab nomads and their cattle would have moved north in order to cross the river before it became full of water.

The two young men reasoned thus, because to the west of them were the Fertit. The Fertit were anti-movement. If the Fertit got them, they would be killed. Likewise, the Arabs nomads, although normally considered friendly, would not spare the life of two lost SPLA soldiers. The Arabs would immediately kill them in order to get the gun they carried and to reduce the number of SPLA combatants. The two were in a fix. If they did not inch their way out carefully and remain undiscovered one enemy or the other would get rid of them.

That night, the two moved very carefully and cautiously. But the forest was as dark as pitch and inhospitable. Before midnight, a heavy rain started to fall. It rained for several hours, till morning. The young men did not take cover from the rain but walked through it till the rain stopped. They reasoned that no Arab or Fertit would be moving or walking in the rain with lightning and thunder.

Sunrise did not bring any change for them. The forest was green, dark and still inhospitable. Birds and thousands of insects could be heard twittering. The grass was between a meter and a few inches high. But the young men were taller than the grass. They could see anywhere around them. No wild animals could be seen. After walking for a few more hours, they came across some monkeys eating some tamarind fruits. When the monkeys saw them, they vanished. The monkeys expected the two to be Fertit hunters, searching for monkeys to kill. The monkeys ran away very fast and were swallowed up by the dark green and luxurious forest. The young men went and helped themselves to some tamarind fruits they could pluck while standing on the ground. Other fruits remained where it was not possible to reach, even when one climbed the tree. Only monkeys could reach them.

It was clean under the tamarind tree. The tree was surrounded by a very large thick bush. The young men entered the bush and spent some hours of daylight there. At about five or six o'clock in the evening the young men started to walk, still heading southward. They were resolved to keep to their previous decision to walk south-ward, maybe for another day before turning eastward. They would know after two days whether the friendly Arab nomads had moved out of the grazing area or if the militia was beaten back the Arabs would have gone back to the river to cross to the northern side.

On that second night the young men walked nonstop. No rain fell again, but in the morning, they became very confused. Although the sun rose as usual, the young men were totally lost. They found themselves among very tall trees, which blocked out the sun. The young men thought they were moving to the west, for they thought the sun rose behind them.

After agreeing among themselves about the position

of the sun and where they were, they decided to take a rest and sleep. Maybe this might clear their minds and by evening the position of the sun would be obvious. They knew the sun rose from the east and goes down in the west, but the tall trees and thick bushes made it difficult for them to know the direction of the sun. Where were they exactly? In the evening they came to terms with their position and that of the sun, but they became hungry and tired, even though they had rested for several hours.

They again started to walk in the direction between where the sun rose from and where it went down. The young men could still see no wild animals. Only birds and a swarm of insects made noise. The birds sang while eating wild fruits on the top of the trees. It was difficult to climb those enormous, tall trees covered by clusters of climbing plants. Everywhere everything was deep green, trees, grass and climbers, all covered by beautiful flowers of every imaginable colour.

Here in this place the grass was becoming taller and thicker. The grass was now up to their shoulders. There was no stagnant water except in some small holes here and there, but they were infested with insects and their larva. The young men had no choice. They took a drink there even if there were insects or their larva in them. It was becoming almost impossible to come by something to eat.

On the third or fourth day, the young men had no notion of the number of days they had spent moving. They walked nonstop for several hours. At about midnight, they found a large track, made either by wild animals or by Arab nomads' cattle. The track was wide, and it headed in both directions, north and south. The two reasoned that a track is like a footpath. It must lead somewhere, either to a village or a river. Our people say, 'When a hyena finds a footpath, it says, a path does not lie. It must lead either to a village or to a river.' Here was a footpath. It must lead to one of these two places, so they followed it.

The rain began to fall again, throughout the night heavily with streaks of lightning and thunder. The rain eased and showered for about two to three hours towards morning hours, but the young men would not stop walking. Early in the morning, the track brought them to a stream full of water, with clusters of papyrus and elephant grass in it. The grass and the papyrus and elephant grass were so tall and thick that a person had to climb a tree in order to see the other side of the stream. To see around them one of them needed to climb a tree. Here, the grass was taller than their height. The vegetation on the other side of the stream was as thick as on the side the young men were. The young men went to the stream and took a drink. They then decided to walk along the bank of the stream to the east, to where the sun rose. No trees grew along the stream. The nearest trees were about two to three hundred meters way.

The sun rose, appearing to them this time mysteriously enormous and several times its normal size as reasoned by the young men.

'Let us move further away from the track,' said Kedit. 'The track could have been made by the Arabs' cattle or wild animals. We don't want either of them to find us.'

So, they walked away from the track for about two kilometers to the east. They went to where the trees were many and with thick bushes under them. The two entered under a thick bush to rest and maybe to sleep. They were hungry and tired. After clearing some space, in order to lie down, Kedit saw smoke rising on the other side of the stream. Kedit told Riel, 'See the smoke up there.'

'See the smoke,' said Kedit again to Riel. 'I think there are people in that place. It might be a village or hunters who have made the smoke. It is said, "There can be no smoke without people."'

The two left the bush and walked cautiously toward the smoke. They knew they could not be seen on the other side unless someone climbed a tree, but why would a person do that? They saw the smoke because of their desperate situation. The smoke did not cease to rise as they walked towards it. 'There must be people there,' Kedit repeated.

After walking for more than two hours, they came opposite to the place of the smoke. The place was on a rise close to the stream about the length of a football field. But between it and the stream, were the tall thick elephant grass and the papyrus. The young men did not know the width and depth of the stream.

The two walked to a nearby bush with a tall tree in the middle. Kedit climbed the tree and saw two young women, cooking. He descended and informed Riel about what he saw. He went up again and directed all his attention and all his faculties to the two women cooking.

Riel lay down and had a nap. He was awfully tired and hungry. After an hour observing the two women, Kedit came down and stealthily inched his way across the thick papyrus and elephant grass. He stealthily went and filled two large barks of a tree with cooked meat and honey. He carried one bark at a time across the stream and returned for the other.

Kedit brought the two barks full of meat and honey to the side they settled on. He put down the two barks and woke Riel. It was a great surprise for Riel. He ran to the stream, washed his face and hands. He came back and both started eating the meat and the honey.

'There are only two young women on that side,' Kedit said.

When the two women finished cooking, they collected all the dirty clothes, maybe of their men. They put the clothes into two basins and came to wash near the stream. They stripped themselves naked. They even removed their underpants. They dived into the water naked. When they finished taking a bath, they sat down on the stones and began to wash.

They got out of the water from time to time, either to spread the washed clothes or ran to play. They ran here and there naked after spreading the clothes. None of them went back to where the hut was. They appeared not to expect any man or any danger to come their way. They remained naked since they came to the stream. They even washed their underpants and put them on the grass far away with the other clothes.

'That's how, I found my way to their compound. There is a lot of meat and honey there. The smoke we saw was for the fire under the *sedab*, for drying the meat. A lot of meat is also cooked, I had to take a piece from here and there. The barks are many and countless.

'Now, we must watch the place for the rest of the day. There may be men elsewhere, who kill the animals and collect the honey. The stream is wide and deep in the middle. The Arabs or whoever is on the other side of the stream will not know that there are people where we are. The grass and papyrus are very tall and thick, it is very difficult to cross. Only a very good swimmer could cross the stream. Natural barriers stand between us and those on the other side of the stream.'

The two women played carelessly, expecting no men or other people to see them. They remained totally naked. They ran or took the washed clothes to the grass some distance away and spread them to dry. Some men might have come with them, even if they were not nearby. The women showed no signs of fear in this dark thick forest by the stream with the tall elephant grass, the papyrus and the creepers.

There was a probability of them having remained for a long time without encountering any danger, either from people or wild animals. The women were used to remaining alone during the daytime. The women threw themselves into the water and ran here and there near their washing place. They never attempted to look back to the compound or to go and see the things left there.

Riel told Kedit to lie down and take a rest. He was going to observe the area across the stream. The time was before midday. Kedit lay down and slept for a short period. While he slept, Riel saw no movement of any kind, people or animals, only the two women remained near the stream. No change occurred in the women's behavior.

Before two o'clock Kedit woke up and told Riel to take a rest. He would keep watch and guard the area. Riel lay down and slept. Kedit climbed the tall tree again. He looked and searched around the place with his eyes. He looked in all directions, east, west, south and north from where they were. He saw no movement of people or animals. All was quiet and calm.

The two women played in their old place after finishing the washing. Most of the clothes were men *jalabias* and long underwear, worn mostly by people of western Sudan and Darfur in particular. The clothes were all spread on the grass near the stream.

When tired, the women sat or bathed themselves on the flat rock, jutting out of the water and the surrounding flat land near the trees. The compound was also on the rock, high above the surrounding area. There were trees west of the compound. The shadow of the trees covered most of the compound by the time the sun went down to the west.

Most of the utensils and other furniture were put in the shadow of the trees. The hut made of twigs and grass was to the east. A lot of firewood was heaped to the south of the compound where the sedab stood. The fire under the sedab had gone out, but the women did not go back to feed it with more firewood. Maybe the scorching hot sun was left to dry the meat during this part of the day.

Besides a lot of meat and honey, the place was clean. Rainwater washed away any dirt or dust, if any, into the stream. The land sloped towards the stream. The women usually swept off the ashes of the fire after completing cooking and from under the sedab. The mats were arranged in two rows.

Some mats were placed after a prayer rug. Other mats were arranged in two rows. One to the west and the other to the east. An open space was left between them. Pitchers filled with water were placed near the prayer rugs on both sides. The prayer rug faced to the east. Some other pitchers were put around the mats.

Kedit observed this arrangement. He suspected the men to be elsewhere, either in the vicinity or in the dark forest. The men might return at any time. He remained alert. About a quarter to two or after two, Kedit saw a line of men. They emerged from behind the thick bushes, west of the compound. They walked in a line, following one another, in an Indian file.

He counted the number. They were thirteen in number.

Each one of them carried a load, either of meat or honey-comb in the bark of a tree. With that load, all had AK47 rifles at their shoulders with two to three magazines strapped to a gun. The guns hung loosely over their shoulders.

The meat and honey were placed on clean rocks in rows. The meat in its order and the honey also in the same way. Some men hung their guns up on pieces of broken dry branches and others placed theirs against the tree. They all began picking up the pitchers and went to wash their hands up to the armpit, faces and feet, all that the Muslims perform when returning home or before prayers, known as *ablutions*.

The Imam called for prayers. All the men stood behind the Imam, and he started the prayers. After some time, the prayers came to an end and one of the men called the women. "Amuna, Amuna, Senuna, Senuna." The women replied in unison, "Naam, naam, naam."

The women ran to where their garments were thrown. They threw on their long garments and ran to the compound. They did not put on their underwear, only long jalabias, and went to serve the men.

The women served a lot of meat, broth and *asida* made of millet. The people of Darfur like asida of millet. It is their main food. The men consumed many bowls of meat and asida. Drinking water was put in skin bags, which hung on the branches of trees. After eating their full, some men rested, and others put more firewood under the sedabs.

The women ran and collected the washed clothes. They

handed each man his clean washed jalabia. After that, the women withdrew to the riverside. The men undressed, put on clean clothes and took rest for a while. The dirty clothes were again heaped up for the women to wash.

The men rested for about an hour and half before returning to where they went to in the morning. They said their prayers. A man called the women again to return to the compound. The man whispered something into the ear of the bigger woman. They all formed a line, the same line they had formed before. Only three persons took guns, three. The other ten AK47's with their magazines were left behind.

The women gathered the dirty clothes, took them to the stream and soaked them in the water. The women went back to the compound, ate their meal and returned to the streamside. They took off their jalabias before they reached the stream, threw them on the grass and jumped into the stream.

CHAPTER ELEVEN

The women played for some time before starting to wash. Kedit woke Riel and told him what he had observed. 'Now it is the two women who are again left alone. The men went back, but I don't know how long they are going to remain away. The men have left most of their guns. We must get them at any cost.'

The young men decided to capture the women first, before taking the guns. Kedit had stolen a knife at the time he stole the meat and honey. He was going to threaten the bigger woman with it if she resisted. Riel was to take care of the younger woman or girl. Riel was to use the gun in case the other woman put up any resistance.

The young men agreed to catch the women and to drag them to where they were before enquiring about who their men were and where they had gone to.

When will they be back?

Kedit led the way, through the thick papyrus and cluster elephant grass. The young men inched their way slowly till they were near the two women.

The women sang while washing. They did not look back or behind them till they were surprised. Kedit caught the older woman first. Riel got hold of the younger one. Kedit showed the knife to the woman and said, 'If you make a sound, you are a dead person.' Riel did the same to the other woman.

Kedit told the women, '... besides, your men have walked back to the forest an hour ago. Only the two of you are left. Follow us to the other side and no harm will befall you.'

The women complied and followed their captors like sheep to the slaughter.

In the middle of the stream, the women had to be supported. It was deep and a person had to swim to get across. The young men swam while supporting their captives above the water.

On the other side, the women were pulled out naked. The elder woman was cut or circumcised while the younger one was not. Both had erect breasts, which pierced the hearts of the young men. The young men were also naked. Riel was circumcised, while Kedit was not. Both eyed each other's nakedness and their private parts.

Kedit pulled the elder woman a few meters away from

Riel who was struggling with the girl. Kedit started to interrogate the woman, while he admired her beautiful breasts and body build. The woman was circumcised, and no part of her private part could be seen at her groin. The young girl's private part was visible at the groin. She was also beautiful. Both young men remained erect. Kedit questioned the woman.

'Who are you and from where did you come?'

'We are Arabs from Darfur. We came here three or four months ago to hunt and to look for honey. Two convoys left for home, taking dry meat and honey.'

'How many men are with you here?'

'Thirteen in number.'

'Where have they gone to?'

'They returned to where they left the meat of animals they killed in the morning before they came back.'

'When are they coming back?'

'They will return between eight and ten o'clock in the evening.'

'Why would they come back that late?'

'Because they are going to skin the animals and perhaps slice some meat, ready to be smoked. After sunset, they will take honey from the bee hive.'

'Are you sure about the time of their return?'

The woman innocently replied, 'I am sure, my husband told me so. However, the men always come back by night, when they have honey to take out of a hive. They told us today's beehive is a very large one. The hive is from the top of a tree down to its bottom. They said the honey from that hive may fill several jerrycans when the juice is squeezed out.'

'What are you called?'

'I am call Amuna'

'What about the other woman?'

Amuna said, 'She is a girl. Her name is Senuna. She is my sister- in-law. My husband is her brother.'

'What do you have in the camp?'

'We have a lot of dry meat, honey, cooked meat and cooked asida of millet.'

'Are there no guns and ammunition?'

'We have. The men left the guns behind. Some are hanging on the branches of the trees and some are placed against the trees with their ammunition in the magazines. The magazines are strapped against the guns. Other bullets are in bags inside the hut.'

'Are there any explosives?'

'What do you mean by explosives?'

'Bullets that can explode or burst when they are thrown at people, like grenades.'

'No, nothing.'

Riel and Senuna faced each other, eyeing themselves angrily and with hate. They were almost at war with one another. They exchanged no words. When Riel cupped her erect breasts, she violently pushed away his hands and pulled herself away from him. She looked wild at Riel. Riel caught her hand strongly and pulled her toward him.

The girl was very attractive, and Riel continued to remain erect. He saw the erect tits and lips of her private part and that stimulated him the more.

Kedit told Amuna that he was going to have sex with her. Amuna shook her head and looked away from him. Amuna said, 'I am a married woman. I cannot lie with any man besides my husband. You are also uncircumcised.'

Kedit said, 'Amuna, if you refuse, I kill you.'

'No. Don't kill me. Do it, but why are you not circumcised like your friend?'

'I am an Agar. I come from where people are not cut. Kedit pulled Amuna further away from Riel and Senuna. He pushed her to the ground and Amuna was receptive. Riel, without saying a word, pushed Senuna down. She resisted. She began to kick Riel and scratched his face and body with her fingers. Riel got angry, cocked his gun and was about to kill her. Amuna intervened and told Riel not to kill her. 'She is young and innocent, Senuna, please go with him. It is better to live than to die, so young as you are.'

Senuna said, 'I am a girl. I cannot have sex before marriage. Who will marry me, if I am found not a virgin?'

Amuna told Senuna, 'You are not cut. When they cut you, the thing will heal and the man would marry you – will find you to be a virgin.'

Senuna complied, but she remained stiff and defiant. She looked at Riel loathingly. She moved away from him when they finished. Riel laughed at her and pulled her to his thighs. She remained sitting there while Riel cupped both her erect tits. She made low sounds, while tears welled out of her eyes.

After some time Kedit and Amuna repeated the act. Amuna enjoyed sex with her partner. They had some friendly low talk before separating from one another. The other warring partners could not hear their low friendly talk. Riel also forced down his partner and had a second round. This time Senuna was somehow induced by courteous touches rendered to her by Riel.

Senuna grasped Riel firmly as soon as they entered into climax. She breathed heavily and was able to catch and looked at her partner's penis. She examined it, after it was pulled out of her. It was the first time she saw a long erect penis before it began to contract. She asked her partner for his name. 'I am called Riel,' she was told.

CHAPTER TWELVE

Riel asked the girl to get up. Senuna rose to her feet to be escorted back to the other side of the stream. Senuna ran to the stream to clean herself and waited for Riel to come. Riel caught up with her. He embraced her and she did not object. She even put one of her arms on Riel's shoulder.

She submitted herself to the man and she allowed Riel to cup one of her erect breasts. They waded in the water hand in hand. But still they exchanged no words, beside the time Senuna asked for Riel's name. In the middle of the stream, Riel pushed Senuna down under the water. She struggled to rise to the surface, but without success. After a few minutes, Senuna gulped in a lot of water down her stomach and she drowned.

Riel pulled the dead body of his partner to where the two washed the clothes. He placed her corpse in such a way she faced upward with her back lying on the rock. He ran back and met Kedit and Amuna coming to the stream hand in hand and laughing.

'Senuna aca mou. Yen aci thou,' he informed Kedit. 'Mou ku ee ting ken.'

Kedit said, 'Wet ace thok, mou ku.'

In the middle of the stream, Amuna went down under the stream not to rise above the water again alive. In a few minutes she was placed near Senuna, also facing upward dead. Both were left there lifeless and naked.

Kedit and Riel rushed to the compound. They collected all the guns left by the poachers. They carried them to the northern side of the stream. The guns were all AK47's. The young men threw the guns on dry ground and returned as quickly as their legs could carry them.

They gathered all the belts and bags full of ammunition and ferried them across to where the guns were thrown. They went back a third time, gathered the ammunition and anything pertaining to war and carried them across the stream.

When all that was used to kill people was brought across the stream, Riel entered the hut. He carried out a thorough search of the hut. Finding no explosives, or money or anything useful except dry meat and honey in jerrycans and plastic drums. The young men poured the honey out and heaped the firewood against the hut.

The meat, which was drying on the sedab, they threw on the firewood. The honeycomb in the barks went to the hut and the firewood. The grass, which lay in bundles, was thrown on all that was heaped against the hut.

The men and women's clothes, drying on the grass, plus the prayer and sleeping mats, were thrown onto the hut for the fire to get rid of. The pitchers and drinking water skin containers went into the hut also.

Cooking utensils, knives, axes and any other things made of metal and which were useful to the poachers, were buried in the deepest parts of the stream. The poachers were left only with what was on them or what they carried or wore. When they returned tonight, they would find a hut in flames and nothing else.

When the young men saw that everything was collected into the hut, they set fire to it. They then swam across the stream. They covered every track they made to the stream. No one could suspect the enemy to have come from across the stream.

The sun was setting. The smoke could not be seen from afar among the tall trees and at dusk. The whole hut and the sedab with their contents were consumed in no time by the fire.

The young men sat down and ate what they brought from the compound. They began to arrange whatever they were able to carry and what was most essential. They were determined to carry all the guns together with their ammunition.

This time Kedit selected one gun for himself. The guns were AK47's made in Iraq. The two were now fully armed. They could easily defend themselves. They had enough ammunition to use. They strapped several belts of bullets all over their bodies. Kedit carried five guns plus the one he had selected to use in case of an attack. Riel carried four plus his old AK47. Each had three magazines full of bullets, strapped at the gun with plastic strings.

The young men made sure there were no rounds left in any of the guns tied. The bags and rounds they contained, which the young men could not carry, were dropped in the deepest part of the stream.

After finishing tying whatever they could carry, the young men disappeared into the thick dark forest or into thin air as no trace of them would be found. They walked a short distance along the stream, which ran from the west to the east. The two headed eastward, which they pictured, could lead them somewhere on the way to Jur and Dinka lands.

However, they did not know what lay ahead of them. They expected to find either Arab nomads cattle camps or Fertit villages. Both were enemies. It was necessary for them to avoid coming into contact with any of the two.

The forests these two young men travelled through, saw many pitched battles, fought between Arab wildlife poachers, or hunters and the forces of Southern Wildlife Conservation. Year after year, the Arabs from Darfur and Kordofan came in large numbers to kill any animals they saw moving.

The Arabs rode on horses, camels and donkeys.

Whenever, they were spotted, the Fertit who lived and hunted in the area reported their presence to the game wardens. The wildlife forces of Bahr el Ghazal region attacked the Arabs. By then Southerners were one people, protecting their wildlife wealth. Most Arab hunters were either ex-soldiers or soldiers on leave. They had no mercy for any animal they found, big or small. Every now and then, they mowed down a herd they found grazing. One time over a hundred buffaloes were killed in a single day. The Arabs ran after the animals using horses.

When the animals become tired, they are machine gunned down. The Arabs dry the meat and carry it to the north on camels or donkeys for sale. It was a yearly routine. The animals' meat was a commodity, which brought wealth to the hunters.

In those yearly skirmishes, one young man distinguished himself among his colleagues. He became a renowned fighter and an exceptional commander of wildlife forces in the field. Although he was not a trained soldier, but a wildlife force warden, his performance in the field was better than those who trained him.

He was brave, a shrewd fighter and an astute planner. Every time he heard the Arabs approaching, he pre-empted the poachers' plan. He killed several of them, took their arms, horses, camels, donkeys and meat. However, the Arab poachers would not be deterred. They were driven to seek wealth wherever it could be found, even if it was at the loss of one's life.

Every dry season, this young man, named Thuc Majok, from Tonj, was a yearly celebrity of the wildlife forces. He came back to Wau loaded with captured guns, horses, camels, donkeys and elephant tusks and meat of every animal living in these forests.

Thuc defected to the SPLA movement at its inception in 1983. He could have become an able commander in the movement had he not disappeared under mysterious circumstances at the hands of the movement's security organs, which were mostly manned by men from Bor. Thuc was a captain in the wildlife forces by the time he joined the movement.

CHAPTER THIRTEEN

Kedit and Riel knew that the Arabs, although termed friendly, would eliminate them in order to take the guns they carried. The Fertit, likewise would do the same, due to their unfounded hatred against the movement, the Jur and the Dinka people. The educated Fertit, who initiated and instituted the militia against the movement, could not tell you why they were anti. The Fertit militia had several names, 'friendly forces', 'peace forces' or 'the Fertit movement for liberation.'

The militia personnel were worse than the Arabs, their masters. Many towns' people, non-Fertit living in Wau disappeared every night, arrested or killed by them. The Fertit were the arms, eyes and ears of the Arabs. They collected information, correctly or falsely and fed it to their Arab masters.

Every night, they rounded up innocent persons and these were taken to the military intelligent cells. Those innocent persons were tortured by the Fertit personnel under the directive of the Arab officers. After torture, those accused innocent persons were handed over for execution. The Fertit soldiers carried out the death sentence.

A few who survived torture had to pay a lot of money to Arab officers in order to survive and be released. The people arrested were never charged for they had committed no offence. Fertit informers fabricated crimes they alleged had been committed. The Fertit wanted to kill as many Dinka people as possible in order to reduce the number of Dinka in general and those in Wau town in particular. They claimed Wau as a Fertit city and so it must be left to them as they envisaged.

CHAPTER FOURTEEN

The young men moved cautiously as soon as they left the area and the compound in flames. They were heavily loaded and weighed down. They covered a few miles then rested. By midnight a heavy rain started to fall. It was a good relief for them. They continued to walk and rest without fear of meeting an enemy. Early next day, while the rain still showered, the young men entered a large bushy area. The showers covered the footprints they made, and they lay down quietly in it. They could not venture out of the bush. But they could do anything in any part of it without being discovered including defecation. Everywhere around the bush was luxuriously covered in green. The grass was up to a few meters tall. Climbers completely covered the bush in a great circle.

The height of the Arabs or their allies, the Fertit, was almost to that of the grass. However, the two young men believed that if they were found for any reason and by any people in search of honey or rodents, they would not blame themselves. Chance had decreed it so. But they would be able to defend themselves. On the other hand, the chances of them being discovered was very remote. Since the time they had walked into this no-man's land, they had seen no people or human footprints and not even those of wild animals.

This was also a period of cultivation. By now the Fertit villagers were occupied working in their fields. Even those who went in search of honey should have returned to the villages. The rains had been early and heavy for this part of the year.

As for the Arabs, they should be moving out of the area. Their cattle do not like tall grass and heavy rain which was falling almost every other day and heavily.

The young men did not keep guard. They both slept under the wet bush. They spread one wet blanket on the wet ground and slept. By early afternoon Kedit climbed a tall tree. He surveyed the whole place looking in all directions. He saw no people or animals moving, except a few monkeys on a tree a quarter or half a kilometer away. The stream still lay to the south, going eastward as it did on the previous day.

Kedit woke Riel and told him, 'We should be moving. I have seen no people so far.' The young men emerged out of the bush and walked, heavily loaded, in the grass as before. The grass along the stream was taller and very thick. They could escape into the stream in case of danger, and no one would find them. The load they carried was heavier than that of the previous day, although nothing had been added to it. Hunger was also beginning to bite them seriously. They exchanged no words, but they were ever alert and determined to move forward.

Before midnight they found a very large track trampled underfoot by Arab cattle. The track headed from the stream toward the north. The young men followed the track. It was like a road, clear of grass and with small shrubs. They walked in it at ease without many obstacles. It was now quite dark, too dark for anybody to see a moving thing or people.

The place was quiet without any wind and no noise could be heard anywhere. The young men walked and rested, walked and rested. They moved again for an hour or more and rested. The load they carried now was very heavy. They rested every hour or less than that.

Around midnight the young men came upon a group of hyenas fighting over a carcass and the bones of a dead cow or two. The young men could not tell when the animal or animals had died. They sat down and rested while watching the hyenas fighting. They agreed not to follow the track anymore. Arab cattle camps could be near if the cow died that day. If it was the previous day or night, why then did the hyenas not find it before today and eat it. The young men were skeptical. Why would the Arabs still remain up to this day in this dense, dark and damp forest?

The young men could not remember the number of days that had passed since they had escaped death by the hands of the Arab militia men. It seemed to them the number of days was more than a week. 'Are the militia men still fighting with our forces or not?' They did not know how far they were from the theater of fighting or when to return to Dinka land. Here they were in enemy territory. One enemy was on the verge of leaving the area, the other was permanently in this place which was their tribal land.

After resting longer than usual they decided to move between the Fertit villages, if they were near, and the Arab cattle camps if those were not far away. The Arabs were to the left and the Fertit to the right. There was a very remote chance of encountering Arabs, but a high probability of entering a Fertit village. The young men did not know how far the Fertit villages were from the main road which ran between Wau and Raga, and also the distance between them and the Fertit villages.

Walking in the grass slowed down their progress. They walked in single file to avoid small shrubs and bushes. The grass was thick even though not taller than previously before they had taken the track.

Hunger was the worst thing, but they would not yield to it. They were even thirsty although they were walking on flat land which could contain water. It was night. They could not see water holes, water holes that contained some water, even if it was not drinkable. Choice bows to necessity. They were bound to drink any water they came across.

Before daybreak they decided to enter any large bush. The probability of walking into a Fertit village was high. Before finding a bush, the young men stumbled on a small pool, full of water. Here, they drank heartily and walked for a distance of about a mile from the water point. Anyone who knew that water was there would come to it to drink. They might be discovered by such a person, if they hid in a bush near a water hole.

Under the bush, they became more cautious. One of them slept and the other kept guard. Kedit slept first. A Fertit searching for honey or small game will at first have to work in his field. At noon he will then go to look for something to kill in the forest for supper. It could be small game, monkeys or rodents, red rats and so on, which are common in the area. Kedit told Riel that he should be the one to keep guard, from midday to late evening, when they would leave their hiding place.

Kedit lay down and slept. In the late afternoon Kedit woke up. He blamed Riel for oversleeping. 'Why didn't you wake me up exactly at noon?' However, Kedit took his position. He climbed a very tall tree and remained up there observing in every direction. Before the sun went down, Kedit saw two persons, walking southward. He did not see where they came from or why they were heading southward. The men carried no guns. It appeared each of them carried a spear, a panga and an axe. They did not look hostile or that they were searching for anything. They followed each other in a straight line, which Kedit perceived as a footpath. The two persons never looked about or around them. They only looked ahead, relaxed, and were involved in conversation. Kedit followed them with his eyes till they were out of sight.

After that, no people or animals were seen. The place remained quiet with a gentle wind blowing from the south to the north. Clouds were visible everywhere in the sky to the far east of where they were. The sun to the west was already blocked out by luxurious green tall trees. The shade of the trees was several hundred meters long stretched along the ground.

At dusk Kedit woke Riel. 'We must be moving.' He told Riel about the men who walked to the south from where they were. The people did not return. He did not even see where they came from. He saw them walking while they were far from them. As it was becoming dark there was no fear of them meeting anybody, or even entering a Fertit village.

The young men were very hungry, but they would not succumb to it. They could not drink two handfuls of water. They said, 'Let us wet our throats and move out of this place.'

They left the bush with heavy loads and bodies aching to the marrow of their bones. Every part of their bodies pained, but young as they were, they would not leave behind any of the things they carried, the guns and the ammunition, which were as dear to them as life itself. The two vowed not to abandon anything unless hunger threatened to deprive them of their lives.

They walked slowly, but sure and alert. They could not remember when they had last eaten. It was now night, and they could not know which tree bore edible fruits. They walked for two hours and by chance found a tamarind tree still full of fruit, in the bright moonshine.

The Arabs and the Fertit had not come across the tree before. However, monkeys which feed on the fruit of tamarind trees, had not ventured here. The young men suspected a Fertit village was nearby. The Fertit do not see eye to eye with monkeys.

The Fertit hunt monkeys for their meat, so the monkeys must keep their distance or hide well from the hunters. Arabs did not come to this place with their cattle or hunt or search for honey and wild fruits. On the other hand, the Fertit do not search for tamarind fruits. Their search is always fixed on monkeys, rodents or honey.

CHAPTER FIFTEEN

The young men picked some fruit which they ate. They rested while eating. The tamarind fruit tastes sour and makes gas in the stomach. The young men were afraid to eat more than necessary of the fruit. They would not be able to walk soundly if their stomachs were full of gas. They ate the fruit to keep them alive. They also knew that they would not get food unless they ventured into a Fertit village and to enter a Fertit village would be very dangerous and not desirable.

The young men continued to walk despite their desperate situation. This time they walked only for half an hour, then rested. Around midnight they suddenly stepped into a clean swept compound with about three huts, built in a circle. They immediately tip-toed across the compound to the east. They were in a Fertit man's compound.

The young men walked for a distance of about the length of a football field. There, they put down the load they carried. They came back and stood on both sides of the largest hut. They listened for some time to ascertain whether there were people inside the hut or not.

Listening for a short time, they heard the door's bolt pulled with a noise. The hut's door made a creak and a man in pajamas emerged. He did not look around but rushed to the end of the compound and urinated.

After completing pissing he turned to go back to the hut. Two guns carried by two young men pointed at his chest and barred him from entering his house. The man was taken aback. He was ordered not to move or make a noise, but to go ahead of them to the east, where the path leads to. The man obeyed the instructions and went along the path, east of his compound.

When the three arrived to where the loads were, the man was ordered to stop. The man halted and waited to hear from his captors. He was mentally confused. What was happening to him appeared as a dream.

He was ordered to step outside the path to the south from where they stood. He again obeyed and went along. They stopped near the load of guns and ammunition placed side by side on the ground.

Kedit interrogated their captive by asking him, 'Who are you and what is this place called?'

'I am called Leo Miskin Khamis. I am a provincial official from Raga on leave in my village.'

'What do you call the village and whose area is it?'

Leo gave a name, somehow called Khor between Rage and Wau.

Was the village in the Belanda area?

Kedit said, 'How far is the road between Wau and Raga, from where we are?'

'It is about three to five miles to the south of us'.

'Which is nearer to us, Raga or Wau?'

'Wau.'

'What about Aweil and Wau from here?'

'I have not been to Aweil before. But the Aweil border is not far from here. It is about six hours to the end of the forest from this village and another six to seven hours walk to Jur border. There is a high ground in the middle of the Toc, almost midway between the Belanda and Jur areas.'

'Did you ever walk there?'

'No. the hunters and the fishermen, who go there to hunt or fish, used to tell me.'

'Are those people still there now?'

'No. Since the arrival of Arab nomads those groups of people left the place. The Jur and Dinka went back to their areas. The Belanda came back. The people did not want the Arabs to take their dry meat or fish by force.'

'Are the Arab nomads still around?'

'No. The Arabs started their rainy season movement back to the north, sometime past. But they came back later for no known reason. They returned to the Toc although heavy rains are falling. However, they have not been seen or heard of for the last three or four days. They might have tracked back. The rains are frequent and heavier in this part of the year.'

'How far is your house from the rest of the village's houses?'

'It is the last one, towards the forest. The next house to mine is about a quarter of a mile or so to the south. The village begins from the road, to where we are now.'

'Mr. Leo, we are heavily loaded with guns and ammunition. We cannot leave them behind. As we have found you, please help us up to the border between the Jur and the Belanda. We may find other people there to help us.'

Leo could not believe his senses. He recalled several harmful actions he had meted out to the two tribes, Jur and Dinka in the past. He thought, 'If I refuse, the young men might kill me. But if I gave in without a word the young men might become happy and allow me to return home.'

He decided not to resist or say anything that could cause the young men to suspect him. His past deeds might not be known to the two young men.

Leo said, 'I can't. I am waiting for a convoy going to Raga within two days.'

Kedit said, 'Don't think we shall leave you behind, Mr. Leo. You are a Sudan Government official. There are other people fighting to free this country from the yoke of the Arabs, and you intend to go back to resume your work with the Arabs. It is not possible. It is either you go with us or else you will not see tomorrow's sunrise. We are not joking or mincing our words.'

Leo Miskin Khamis uttered words no one heard. Riel tied nine guns together and ordered Leo to pick them up. Riel had to help him with the load. He was asked to lead the way up to the border, which he said was six hours walk.

Heavy clouds had already gathered in the sky. The path entered straight into the forest. Tall grass, thick bushes and very tall trees became more and more abundant the further they walked. They could not see a few meters away from the path. After walking for less than an hour a heavy rain started to pour down in great thick sheets of water.

Leo wanted them to go under a bush to avoid the thick sheets of water pouring down on them. The young men objected. They rested in the path, sitting while the rain fell. They walked again in it. There was also a lot of lightning and thunder. Leo was afraid walking while exposed in the thunderstorm. To his way of thinking lightning strikes people moving in the open. They could be struck by lightning which had become frequent in the sky since the rain started. The red light of lightning flickered across the sky from one end of it to the other.

The rain fell for several hours. It stopped at dawn when the travelers were approaching the end of the forest. Two bushes stood ahead, isolated to the right. The young men could see the Toc as far as their eyes could reach.

A group of trees stood in the middle of the Toc. Leo told the young men, 'Those trees stand on a high ground, frequented by all the tribes coming to hunt or fish. The stream is behind the trees on the Jur side.'

'The stream is always full of fish. Several people spend dry season there to fish. It is when the Arabs come that they leave the place. The Arabs are always armed, and they use force to loot the people. So, when they come to graze their cattle, the hunters and fishermen take home all the meat they have dried. The Arabs are left alone in the Toc to graze their cattle, to hunt or fish. But they don't fish because the stream is full of water and is deep. However, the Arabs kill a lot of wild game.

'In the past, wildlife conservation force fought pitched battles with the Arabs and drove them away. Now, no one hinders the Arabs' movements or the killing of the animals in great numbers. They can now kill the animals at will.

'At times the soldiers from Wau or Raga, when on leave, send for their tribesmen to come and hunt. The Arabs who came here this year are poorly armed. They hide their guns when they see people. But those who come from Wau and Raga are always heavily armed. They have not appeared this year.'

Leo was ordered to lead the way to the far isolated bush. They were to spend daylight hours under that bush. Maybe the Arabs might come with their cattle to graze. Leo led the way. He put down the load and lay down at once without a word on the wet soil. His pajamas were still soaked and dripping with water. The sun began to rise in the right direction for the first time as the young men looked at it.

Riel told Kedit to sleep. He would wake him before midday. Leo was so tired that he began to snore at once.

Leo's shoulders and head began to blister. Stains of blood appeared on his pajamas. He was not used to carrying heavy loads on his head or shoulders.

After two hours, Kedit woke up. He immediately climbed a tall tree and started to survey the whole area with his eyes. The grass was of the same height and there were no other obstacles or trees to obstruct his vision.

Kedit saw no movement of cattle or people. A few wild animals grazed here and there, several kilometers apart to the far side, south of where they were. The Toc was as clear as the sky. Kedit remained up the tree for more than an hour.

Riel lay down and slept. Leo remained stretched on the ground like a piece of wood. He remained asleep on one side without turning. His body ached to the marrow of his bones. He did not open his eye till he was awakened.

While Kedit remained on the tall tree and saw no movement, he decided that they should be moving. The group of trees in the middle of the Toc appeared to be near, but they were tired, exhausted and hungry. It might take them more hours than anticipated to reach it. It was already afternoon. Their movement would be slowed by hunger, tiredness and exhaustion.

The sun was hot, the air was thick and humid, and no wind blew. They moved at a snail's pace. No one talked. When one of them put down his load, the others follow suit. None made a request of the others to rest. There was no cover in the sky from the fierce scorching sun and the thick windless air. The three men sweated out to the last drop of water. But after taking some water not a drop of perspiration would appear on the skin. After more than six hours they arrived at the group of tall trees standing on high rocky ground in the middle of the Toc.

CHAPTER SIXTEEN

No person understands the work of nature. No stone or rock can be found in a Toc. How a rock appeared in this place is a mystery. The place was clean, and the trees were arranged by nature in an orderly way. They stood tall and erect, along the raised rock and in a line all around as if planted.

There was no vegetation underneath the trees. The roots of the trees seem to have gone below the rock. No roots appeared above the ground, as the place was rocky. The raised and rocky area was about the size of two football fields put side by side and somehow almost square in shape.

A deep stream ran below the high ground to the east. At the far end of the ground to the east a fish bird called *kuei* (that is 'bald eagle') was struggling, pulling a large fish from the stream to the dry high ground. The young men saw the bird. They looked at it struggling hard with the fish. They allowed the bird to pull the fish far away from the shore of the stream. The bird did not see the three persons.

After pulling the fish a meter or more away from the stream, the young men again waited, allowing the bird to extricate its claws from the fish. The bird rested for a while before starting to eat. Kedit watched the bird intently and picked up a piece of wood, shouted at the top of his voice and walked fast towards the bird. He threw the piece of wood at the bird with a loud shout. The bird had no time to react. It flew away seeing Kedit moving towards it. The bald eagle is a very clever and selfish bird. If it had time, it would have pulled the fish back into the water. It could not fly away with the fish because it was too heavy to carry. Also, the bird did not see the people when it was struggling with the fish. If it had, it would have pulled out its claws and left the fish in the water.

It was a big fat fish. Kedit asked Riel to help him carry the fish to where they sat in order to cook it. The place known as high ground had everything in it. There were cooking utensils, firewood and even a box of matches, kept in one of the cooking saucepans. The place was clean as if it was always swept. Leo told the young men that all those who hunt or fish and stay in the place must leave it as clean as when they found it. Hunters and fishermen mostly spend dry season in this place. None of them begrudged the other. Here, they were all Southerners not tribesmen. They hunted and fished together. Most of the items in this place were commonly owned. Whatever a person brought here was shared and most of them were nonperishable items. The items were left in the place when the owner went away to be used by other persons coming later.

Although tribal divisions existed or were created by the townspeople (mostly by educated people), here the people were all brothers. The divisions of the townspeople had not filtered down to these people and affected the way they lived. Anybody coming to hunt or fish had to abide by the norms and customs of the people staying in the high place in the Toc. The people who came with tribal divisions were asked to evacuate the place and go and practice their ideas where they came from.

The Arabs encouraged tribal sentiments among the Fertit tribal groups, especially among the educated people. The Fertit were armed and encouraged to clear away the Jur and Dinka people still residing in Wau town and in any other towns where the Fertit were the majority.

Abu Gurun Abdalla Abu Gurun instituted, armed and supported the Fertit militia, under the leadership of Tom el Nur. Abu Gurun helped the militia with all the arms they needed. He also preached the evils the Dinka people meted out against the Fertit. He preached that the Dinka and Jur people must be driven away from Wau.

Having acquired the necessary arms, many young Fertit

men and women were enlisted in the army and the militia. Daily attacks were launched against the Jur and the Dinka township. The city of Wau was divided into townships by the militia. The Fertit, the Arabs and the Falata plus other non-Nilotics had a township of their own. The Dinka and the Jur were forced into one township north-east of Wau.

Abu Gurun would allow the Fertit soldiers to join their brothers and sisters who attacked the unarmed and unwanted people. The Falata youth and their elders had also enlisted in the Fertit militia. When an attack was launched, the town's population separated according to zones or townships. The Arabs who had businesses in the centre of the city, left the place of their work by four o'clock every evening or when an attack was imminent or mounted. They went to support the Fertit militia.

At night, the Fertit zone was alive with people, buying and selling. Parties were held there while the other zones remained in darkness and in anguish. Whenever the Fertit militia saw light coming from a house in a zone not their own, that house was bombed.

For other people to be saved they were to remain in darkness and without moving from dusk to dawn. The Fertit liberation youth moved at will. Their assignment was to kill the Dinka and their ally the Jur. Those tribes were to be forced out of Wau town. The town of Wau was claimed by the Fertit.

Grenades and other explosives were issued to the Fertit militia to use at night in the Dinka and Jur zone. There were no Jur or Dinka people elsewhere in the Fertit, Arab and Falata zones. The city of Wau was divided, Beirut style, with a road dividing the two areas.

All the other Nilotic tribes were forced to move to the Dinka zone. They were their kith and kin. They were considered to be enemies because they were supporters of the SPLA movement. Even the soldiers in the army who were not from the people friendly to the Fertit would not venture into their area.

The Fertit were above the law. The Fertit militias were allowed to kill a Dinka or a Jur and they would not be arrested or charged by the police. A Fertit militia man or a soldier would not be taken before any court of law. 'Abu Gurun is the law.' Several members of the militia were generals and officers in militia ranks and uniforms.

No one had the guts or authority to question them for any crime committed, especially if it was meted out against the Dinka and the Jur. The militia men were free to rob and to loot properties of the non-Fertit during broad daylight. The security organs had no right to stop or question their actions, unless the property robbed belonged to a Northern Sudanese. The militia had no power over Northern Sudanese nationals.

Most Fertit young, including students, mature schoolboys and girls, officials, teachers, traders and members of the organized forces, police, wildlife and prison, were all drafted into the militia. Any mature person who did not enlist into the militia forces was considered to be an enemy or a renegade. Such a person was subject to lynching. All officials of every grade and position performed their official assigned duties during work time and went to launch an attack against the Dinka and Jur quarters during or after working hours.

On the other hand, the Dinka policemen, prisons and wildlife warders defended their people. Wau became a small Beirut most afternoons when the militia launched attacks in order to drive out the Jur and Dinka people from the town.

Several Dinka and Jur policemen lay down their lives in defence of their people. But they had no guns or ammunition. The police and prison warders used old British Mark 3 rifles, *abu-ashara*. Those rifles were heavy to carry and they had no ammunition. The rifles had been replaced several years back, but the army still had the ammunition in their stores.

The wildlife forces had wildlife Magnum guns, but without ammunition also. However, the rounds for these guns were available in the army stores. The Dinka residents in the town collected money and illegally purchased the rounds. Abu Gurun was always in a fix. He wondered, 'Where do those forces get their ammunition to repulse every Fertit militia attack?'

Abu Gurun might have been or might not have been aware that the forces in Wau used the same stores from which he supplied arms and ammunition to the Fertit militia forces. The men in the logistics department were not all anti-Dinka and there were other Nilotics. Those men also wanted to get rich and so they did in the same illegal way Abu Gurun was enriching himself.

Abu Gurun was enriching himself by felling most teak plantations near Wau. Abu Gurun depleted the plantations for several miles on Tonj Wau and Wau Raga roads. He employed the army and the Fertit militia to chop down every mature teak tree.

The logs were transported to the north in militia planes when the trains stopped coming to Wau. He also constructed two furniture workshops in Wau and Khartoum. Probably some big personalities in Khartoum and in the army were behind the business and collaborating with Abu Gurun. Abu Gurun was never questioned even when a C130 military plane caught fire in midair carrying teak logs. The logs, a few passengers plus the crew all got burnt and all perished. The plane burned to ashes. No enquiry was carried out and Abu Gurun was never questioned.

Several Fertit carpenters were employed to saw the wood and to make furniture for Abu Gurun. Ready-made furniture was also transported to Khartoum for sale and he gave some to personalities who were behind the project.

Abu Gurun came to Wau to kill and to loot. He instilled fear in all the inhabitants living in Wau town. He killed at random and looted at will. Abu Gurun first started to loot by first dismantling Wau sawmill known as Russian sawmill. The sawmill was constructed with Russian aid.

Next were the two factories at the periphery of Wau, known as Beer and Fruit factories.

Most of the machinery in those factories and the sawmill were transported to the north. Abu Gurun next turned to government cars and vehicles. Many of them were in good working condition but could not move because they lacked fuel. It was only the army which had fuel. Abu Gurun towed all those cars and vehicles to the army headquarters in Girinti and they were transported to Khartoum to be sold there. The proceeds from the sale went straight into Abu Gurun's pocket.

Abu Gurun was regarded as a father and benefactor by the Fertit people, including the highly educated persons. They called him *Abui*, the father of their liberation, even though the term was often contradicted. On the troop carriers was written the words *nik el Fertit, wa aktul el Dinka* – 'Fuck the Fertit and kill the Dinka.' The educated Fertit read those words clearly, but they put their heads in the sand. The Dinka and Jur were their worst enemies. They had to be eliminated by big brother Abu Gurun and his army.

CHAPTER SEVENTEEN

Riel and Kedit were very happy. Luck gave them a big fish which the bird had pulled out of the stream. The young men immediately lit a fire, cut the fish into some portions and placed it on the fire to boil. It was very fat and its oil covered the surface of the soup and the flesh beneath.

There were several dishes and even salt stowed away in the utensils. After boiling it nicely, the young men decided to sip the soup first while it was still hot. They woke Leo who was lying flat on the ground. He was offered a bowlful of soup. Leo took a few mouthfuls of soup and began to feel better. He opened his eyes and looked searchingly at the young people. Before this, the two were enemies like the rest of their tribesmen. Leo uttered the words, 'Thank you,' and went on to take the soup in small draughts.

Leo felt relieved, both of body ache and hunger. He recalled their first encounter and the precarious walk and the heavy load which he carried. After all, the young men were not as unfriendly as he had imagined. All three completed taking the soup in the bowls. They rested for a while then started to eat the fish flesh.

The three men could not eat much. They decided to warm the fish when they felt the need to eat. They were full and there was no more thought of hunger for they were soon attacked by swarms of mosquitoes, such swarms as they had never experienced before. Kedit and Riel climbed onto the boughs of trees, two meters above the ground. Leo lay flat and slept like a log of wood, mosquitoes or no mosquitoes. However, within a short time, a heavy rain started to fall. Again, this rain fell in large thick sheets of water. The rain was so heavy that it appeared as if the earth and the sky merged into one.

Leo never minded about the rain or water, and neither did the young men. The young men remained awake on the boughs of the trees throughout the night till morning. Leo lay uncomfortably and tried to sleep. His pajamas were a mess of dirt. He had no spare clothing like the young men.

However, the young men thought they were soldiers and were accustomed to conditions like this. They kept awake on the boughs of trees with the filthy and dirty clothes they had on, the same clothes they were wearing when they got separated from their main force. The two changed their old dirty uniforms and put on the Arabs' clean jalabias in the morning. Each of them had also taken a number of jalabias when they left the poachers' camp which they set on fire.

This day they were between Jurland, which was friendly and the Fertit area from where an enemy might come. Their attention was to be focused on the enemy area. But all who came to this place were expected to be friendly. A person coming with bad intentions was never welcome. However, the Toc was as clear as the sky. Any person approaching or an animal was visible to the eye as far as eyesight reached. The young men saw some wild animals grazing far away towards the Fertit area. Friendly Arabs were not expected to come back here to graze their cattle. The rains had become heavier these last two days, and the Toc was almost flooded with rainwater.

After sunrise, Kedit told Leo to wash his dirty pajamas and to remain in his underwear. 'We are to take rest in this place till the following morning.' There were small pieces of soap among the utensils. They took those pieces and washed their dirty clothes.

The two young men could face any danger, if it ever came or they would cross to the other side of the stream in case they were overwhelmed. The stream had overflowed its banks. As Leo had told them, the stream was deep. A tall person, who cannot swim, would not cross it, let alone short stature persons or ones who cannot swim like the Arabs.

Also, if they were to see many people coming from far, they would move out of the place for protection. So, their decision to remain in the place was well thought out. They were also going to wash their military uniforms and put on the wet jalabias. The hot sun would dry them on their bodies.

The young men warmed the fish of the previous evening and ate it. In the stream were several fishing lines placed there and left when the last fishermen went away. The owners never returned to check them. After eating, Riel and Kedit stood on the high ground to survey the stream and beyond it. They saw several lines moving up and down with a catch. One of them went into the stream and pulled out several fish which they intended to consume and the best type of fish too.

The young men emptied the saucepan and placed several nice fish in it and began to cook them. While the fish was boiling, they washed their clothes and put on the Arab jalabias. The sun began to get hot before ten o'clock. All their clothes dried and Leo had to put on his pajamas. Each of them ate when he felt hungry and lay down on the bare rock which jutted out of the high ground and slept.

CHAPTER EIGHTEEN

B y midday, the young men were fresh again. Both started to clean and grease their guns. Kedit had never used the gun he selected for himself. It was brand new as were the other guns. Leo went back to sleep. He was still tired and wounds were visible on his head and shoulders. He had alternated between carrying the guns on his shoulders and head.

Kedit climbed a tree facing the Fertit area. He saw two animals walking towards the high ground. The animals walked in a line following one another. He suspected people to be riding them. No other animals came behind them or elsewhere, near or far, to the right or left. He observed the animals attentively.

When the two were midway, he was sure no other

animals were following from behind. He turned to the Jur side, but no moving animals could be seen. A few wild animals were grazing far away to the south. Kedit turned again to where the two animals were approaching. He identified the animals. They were two horses, maybe ridden by two riders. He suspected the riders to be Arabs. Southerners do not usually ride horses. Perhaps a few of them might be able to ride horses. The Fertit were like other Southerners, who knew very little about horses. If the two riders were Southerners, they must be policemen or game wardens searching for Leo, if they suspected him to have moved this way.

Kedit descended from the tree. He informed Riel in a whisper. 'Two riders are approaching us. Let us get rid of them at once, be they Southerners or not. The horses have loads on them, plus the two riders. Get rid of the first one and I will take care of the second.'

The two riders dismounted from their horses, caught them by the reins and pulled them along with the ropes. The two men walked leisurely without suspecting any danger. The place appeared very quiet, deserted and without a living thing to be seen. Kedit and Riel had placed themselves in such a way that they could not be seen. Leo was fast asleep at the far end of the high ground.

The two Arab riders were very short. They could not see anything at the far end before climbing the high ground. Before the leading person could approach the high ground, Riel knocked off his head. The second rider tried to take cover but there was nothing and nowhere to go to do that. Kedit also blew off his head. The two fell still holding the reins of the horses. The horses moved away from the fallen riders.

Leo got up, very much alarmed and frightened. He nearly ran to the stream. The young men had to shout to him aloud to stop and not to get drowned in the stream. He stopped a few yards away from the bank of the stream, shaking all over with fear. Kedit asked him to come back. He told him they had shot two Arab horse riders.

Leo returned to where the young men stood. He caught the horses and tied them to a tree. Each horse carried a load. The horses were handsome and well cared for. They were used to being ridden because they remained calm. Kedit pulled off the loads from the horses. The loads turned out to be guns and ammunition. Each horse carried sixteen guns, eight on each side and a *mudfa* (field gun). The horse riders also carried some food items for their sustenance.

When the dead riders were searched, documents were found. The two came from Wau garrison. Their ID's indicated that. The letters or writing found in their pockets were in the Arabic language.

Kedit took the written material to Leo to read. Leo found that the two were from Wau. They were going on leave to Darfur. They were supposed to have left with the convoy going to Raga which Leo was waiting for and missed.

Further in the written material they carried, Leo discovered that they were bringing the guns to their relatives, the

Arabs, who are said to be friendly to the SPLA movement. They had heard in Wau that their tribesmen had no arms to defend themselves. The guns they carried were left in SPLA custody near the border, before they entered the movement's zone.

The coming government offensive would destroy and dislodge the movement's forces from the area. Thus, the arms of their people would also be taken by the government forces and their militia collaborators. The government forces and the militia would turn against their people here in the grazing areas, or when they went back to Darfur. The Sudan Government Army and the militia are their sworn enemies. Unless they are armed, they and their cattle will not be saved. Government Arab tribes' supporters were permitted to fight them and to take their cattle by force. Their people had allied themselves to the enemy of Allah and the nation. The two unfortunate riders were trying to find their tribesmen's cattle camps. They were told by the Fertit they had asked that their people had either moved to Jurland or Dinka areas who are their friends. The Arab cattle camps left the Fertit area almost a week before the horse riders came in search of them.

The young men got thirty two AK47 guns, two mudfa and large quantities of rounds. Each of the riders had about five thousand dinars tied to his body, plus some canned food and biscuits. Each of them carried a water container, some clothes and mosquito nets.

The loads were not heavy. The horses carried them with

ease. Leo asked the young men to allow the horses to go and feed nearby. But Kedit and Riel knew nothing about horses. They told him to go and release the horses to go to graze near the place. Leo tied a rope to one of each horse's front feet and fastened it to the other foot behind. The horses were then allowed to graze.

The young men were extremely happy. Their arms cache was by now large. They also had the means to transport them. But how? The young men were not aware that a horse could swim till Leo told them. A horse can swim with a load on its back, if it is not too heavy.

It was news to the young men. It was so wonderful they remained in the place another day. They never expected such an opportunity to come their way. There were plenty of fish also to feed on. They became very contented and almost forgot their ordeal of a few days past.

Tomorrow they would leave the place with two horses to carry all their guns and ammunition. They cooked fish and asida made of millet flour, captured from the two soldiers who were killed. Sugar and other food items were found in the small bags carried by the soldiers. This added to what was to eat on the way back to their unit.

But what were they going to do with Leo? Leo had helped them. He was kind, useful and submissive. Would they allow him to return to his family from here or take him along or should they kill him?

'Let us leave it for the night and tomorrow morning. Maybe something will tell us what to do with him. He is a Southerner although his tribesmen are hostile to the movement,' said Kedit to Riel.

The young men took turns to sleep. They feared Leo who remained awake most of the evening hours. Leo knew something about horses. He could jump on a horse and ride off. Each of them remained awake and vigilant, scanning the whole Toc from time to time. The moon shone bright. One could see as far as the eye could reach.

The young men also suspected that other horsemen might come or the fishermen, who left because of the Arabs, might return, since the Arabs had gone back. Some of the fishermen and hunters earned their living by fishing or hunting.

Hard working persons would not leave their fields to come to fish in the stream. But lazy ones or those who trade, selling dry fish or dry meat might return to carry on with fishing and hunting. Every possibility should not be ruled out. Other daring soldiers might turn up this way bringing help to their people. Arab soldiers also trade in arms. They sell guns and ammunition to the SPLA soldiers. On the other hand, SPLA soldiers do the same. Several SPLA soldiers lost their lives because they sold guns to the Arabs, including their personal guns, or took bribes in order to render secret information to the enemy.

Once a soldier was executed instead of a killer he had allowed to escape, twenty-four hours before the execution was due to take place. The killer, the escapee, had killed an innocent civilian for only fifty dinars. The killer saw the deceased pocketing the money. He went and waited for him in the way. Without asking the man, he fired at him and killed him instantly. The sound of a gunshot was heard. The soldiers rushed to the scene. They met the killer running, trying to escape.

He was apprehended and he confessed to killing the man. Why? because of the money. The soldier was sentenced to death by firing squad. His relatives paid five cows to a guard to permit their convicted relative to escape. The guard received five cows and by night he let the murderer escape. The sentence was to be carried out in the morning of the following day.

In the morning the criminal was nowhere to be found. The guard was asked about the killer. He gave lame excuses pertaining to the escape. Other prisoners who had been convicted of some minor crimes had not attempted to escape. The incident was reported to the authorities concerned. The authorities' instructions were to kill the guard or guards who let the murderer escape. The act was found to be the work of one man. He confessed and asked for pardon. He said he would not repeat it.

No pardon was granted. The punishment meted out to him would be a lesson to all those who sell arms to the enemy or those who receive bribes. The following morning the culprit was executed. He acknowledged his wrong-doing. He allowed the murderer to escape for only five cows. He lost his life due to greed giving his own life for the cows given to him.

The guard thought that no punishment would be meted out to him. Some guards had previously committed the same offence and were left unpunished. He attributed his situation to bad luck. The movement set down his case as an example to dissuade other guards or soldiers from making the same mistake. The guard was shot dead. The cows were given back to the murderer's relatives with a stern warning.

CHAPTER NINETEEN

Leo told the young men at the beginning of their journey from his home that it was about six hours walk to the bamboo grove in Jurland. The bamboo grove was visible from the high ground. But now it took longer than expected.

The three started walking from the very early morning hours. They should have arrived at the bamboo grove by noon, but by late evening the grove was still some distance away.

Leo could not walk well and fast enough. He was bogged down by recalling his past deeds. He was sure someone would recognize him when he appeared among SPLA soldiers. Although he gave a name, not his own, to the young persons, someone who knew him from before would call him with his real name. This name is anathema to the Dinka and Jur people, especially those who had left Wau. Leo was not his real name. The real one, the awful one, Pio is hated even by the unborn.

The young men did not think to tell Leo to hurry or walk faster. The bamboo grove was not near enough to reach before sunset. Leo looked sick and in pain. He gurgled in his throat as if swallowing or pissing something away.

Leo's thoughts turned to his past deeds. Thinking hard and recalling all that he had done nearly prevented him from putting one foot before another. He was heading to Dinkaland where people he had tortured or maimed were likely to recognize him.

Leo recalled the first attack on Dinka and Jur people in Bussere. All that the Fertit laid their hands upon were murdered. All their businesses and houses were ransacked, looted and set on fire. Only one house was left. It was turned into militia offices. Leo thought, 'The few fugitives who might have escaped, if they see me … that will be the end of me.'

The second incident was when the militia under his command attacked all the Dinka residents among the Fertit houses. Several occupants of those residences perished. A few fugitives who had been forewarned by some of their Fertit friends escaped but the furniture and other belongings in the houses were left to the mercy of Fertit fighters. All those houses among the Fertit homes were set ablaze. The houses built with bricks and stones were razed to the ground.

Another atrocity was the cutting down of four young boys who went to visit a relative admitted in Agok Leprosy Hospital. The boys were cut to pieces as if their flesh was to be cooked. The hospitalized relative suffered the same fate as the boys at the hands of the Fertit militia. The militia had no mercy.

'It was me,' thought Leo, 'who threw grenades into several houses in the Dinka and Jur areas. Only I knew how to use grenades till the time I taught the Fertit youth how to throw a grenade.'

He, Leo, with most militia fighters, accompanied convoys going to Tonj, Rumbek and even Gogrial. In every convoy he made sure that several villages enroute were destroyed and the cattle and goats were taken. The militia fighters were free to do as they desired.

Leo recalled these many diabolical deeds he had carried out in the past. He crowned them with the partition of Wau town and the planting of a land mine which killed Dr. James Akile with all the theatre technicians on their way to Agok Leprosy Hospital.

Dr. Akile's death was a great lost which Leo did not anticipate. Dr Akile's death prompted the Dinka and Jur people to cross the dividing line in great numbers in order to mourn his death and to witness the burial of whatever was collected of all their remains. The Landcruiser the landmine blew up was shattered to pieces with all its occupants. The Dinka and Jur people did not care what the Fertit militia might do to the multitude who crossed the green line. Dr. James was mourned by all the communities which he diligently served without distinction.

Dr. James Akile never left Wau civil hospital. He stayed every time a fight erupted between the Fertit militia with the support of the Sudan Government Army and Dinka and Jur policemen. Wounded Fertit fighters were taken and treated in the military hospital while the other people were attended to by Dr. James and Dr. Michael Milli, the two of them Fertit by tribe. The two never shied away from their medical ethics. But their work was hated by the Fertit because they were regarded as renegades helping the enemy.

CHAPTER TWENTY

However, in retrospect the Dinka have never been kind to themselves either. During Anya-anya One, some Dinka persons killed more of their own people than those killed by the Fertit.

Three persons readily come to mind: Teny Deng Santino, Adhal Longar Salva, and Ring Bol Benjamin. The atrocities these three committed were worse than what Leo had done so far. However, the Dinka people promptly forgot all the bad deeds meted to them by those three Arab stooges.

The three formed a political party and named it 'Unity' after the fall of Abouol's military regime in 1964. All the northern parties supported the so-called Unity party one hundred percent. The north poured a lot of money into it in order to bribe the ignorant and hungry southerners to support a party which called for a united Sudan.

The Unity Party and SANU (Sudan Africa National Union) inner faction frustrated other Southern parties during the Round Table Conference. The northern parties adhered to the call for unity by the Unity Party. The conference ended in failure because the party of those three persons and SANU of William Deng Nhiel called for unity and federation respectively. The other southern parties, SANU outer faction of Aggrey Jaden and Southern Front called for self-determination. The northern parties exploited the differences within the southern parties in rejecting the call for federation or self-determination.

After the conference, the three northern stooges flew to Wau one July morning. Their presence in Wau, an order given by the stooge leader to the Arab army, triggered the Wau massacre of 1965. Many leading Dinka officials, politicians and other leading personalities were murdered in a house where a wedding party was taking place. In the morning, the three hailed the death of all those people. Among the dead were some of their relatives and friends. The three regarded the dead as supporters of federation and self-determination, which they detested bitterly. Two days earlier, Juba was shattered and her innocent citizens were massacred by the Arab and Islamic Army.

Not satisfied with this, the three went in convoy to Aweil. The army in Wau had placed a special squad at their disposal to guard them and to take them to any town of their choice. The leader of the three was from Aweil.

Aweil was set in turmoil on their arrival. A few officials

escaped death by running away from the town at night or before the death squad reached their homes. The following night, the few officials and non-Unity Party supporters who continued to linger about in Aweil town were done away with.

The people of Aweil became polarized between the supporters and non-supporters of Unity Party. The parish priest of the Catholic Church had escaped to Wau, by another route, the day before the convoy arrived in Aweil.

When much destruction and death had been committed against the innocent citizens of Aweil town, the convoy returned to Wau arriving in the evening. Unfortunately, they met Fr. Barnaba Deng's car, driven by him going to give the last sacrament to a dying Christian in Hila Fahal. Fr. Barnaba was the Catholic Parish Priest of Aweil.

Fr. Barnaba's car was stopped by order of the party leader. Fr. Barnaba was pulled out of the car by an Arab soldier and shot dead. His corpse was left lying on the road near the car and the convoy proceeded leisurely to the Riverside Rest House as if nothing had happened.

The next destination, the convoy of the three went to, was Tonj. The second man came from there. Upon their arrival, the town of Tonj was cordoned off and set on fire. A few officials and other citizens who had left the town after hearing of the Wau massacre were saved. Those who did not leave before the arrival of the convoy lost their lives, headed by the Inspector of Education Luis Nyok Kuol. Tonj town was scoured to the last man.

William Deng Nhial came from Tonj. He had the largest number of supporters there. So, all his supporters and non-Unity Party supporters were to be silenced if they had not escaped. Only Unity Party supporters and citizens from northern Sudan were left or remained in the town.

After making sure no suspected opposition persons or officials, anyone who might call for federation or self-determination remained, the convoy again left for Rumbek. Before the convoy came to a halt Rumbek was set ablaze. There was shooting all over the town.

A prison officer was attacked and killed by his own men from the prison force. He was a southerner and a supporter of Southern Front, a party hated most by the Arabs from the north. The prison forces were mostly from northern Sudan, Arabs and Muslims. Our African brothers from northern Sudan were Muslims and that logically, according to them, entitled them to be called Arabs.

Fr. Arkangelo Ali, a Catholic Priest was murdered in his church with all the faithful who were found in the church's compound. The church's premises were ransacked by the northern soldiers, who lived a short distance away from the church area. Most of the inhabitants of Rumbek had fled from the town when they heard about the atrocities carried out in Wau, Aweil and lastly Tonj. Only northern Sudanese people and Unity Party supporters remained in the town.

Yirol was the last town to the east that the convoy went to. Not satisfied with this havoc at their bloody hands,

Yirol too went up in flames and several innocent citizens were killed. But here most of the town's leading personalities, including the Inspector of Local Government left the town before the convoy's arrival. The inspector left in his official car. When the fuel ran out, he walked the rest of the distance on foot to safety. He remained in hiding for almost a month, before he was smuggled by the local people into a steamer going to the north. The inspector was dressed in the short *cop weng* jalabia. His clothes, including his official uniforms and badges, were hidden till he had left what was known as the southern border. The inspector put on his official dress one early morning in Kosti, the last stop of the steamer. The people who were used to seeing him and interacting with him were surprised and puzzled.

When the convoy returned to Wau from Yirol, Gogrial remained as the last destination. The third person of the three came from Gogrial and especially from Twic. But the people of that town had learned a great deal from what had taken place in the other towns. The chiefs, elders and the inhabitants of the town received the convoy with pomp and music, sang songs in praise of the three, especially their leader and the party. The party leader became very happy and praised Gogrial citizens for their support of Unity party and its leadership.

However, many government officials left Gogrial town for the countryside after the Wau massacre. The majority of the people who had lost their lives in the wedding party were from Gogrial district. The citizens who knew the mindset of the three persons had taken advantage of the time that elapsed while the convoy went to other towns.

At a rally the three conducted the following day, one of them explained to the public listening the sentences which would be meted out to the enemies of unity of the country. He said that non-supporters of unity would be given a punishment worse than death.

All the listeners were surprised. Nothing could be worse than death. Death is the last stage of any living thing, including humans. But the three, whether through arrogance or ignorance, went ahead to explain their newly devised idea which they regarded as worse than death.

One of them explained, 'All those against unity of the Sudan will be collected and packed in an airplane and dropped when the plane is several thousand feet above the ground. The other punishment will be to tie all those opposed to unity under cars. The cars will then be driven at high speed over long distances and for long periods.'

To the audience those actions were worse than death. No one could contradict them. They had all the airs and graces. What the three said was hailed and applauded by the Gogrial town residents. The three were more than satisfied.

The people of Gorial had their own massacre before the fall of Aboud's regime in 1964, during late September or early October of that year. Anya-nya One fighters attacked every village station in the whole district. All the traders in those areas came from the north and called themselves Arabs or *Jalabas*.

During the Anya-nya attack, many northern traders lost their lives and property. Those who escaped, flocked to Gogrial town, the only place that was left under government control.

Upon their arrival and after relating what had happened to them and to those who would not come, the police and the army rounded up every local citizen they saw moving. The culprits, as the police and the army termed them, were starved for almost a week without food or water.

One late evening either in late September or early October 1964, those unfortunate victims were marched two or three kilometers out of the town. They were told to sit down and then sprayed with machine gun bullets till they all died. Between seventy to eighty persons perished. Their dead bodies were heaped up in the form of a meter of logs, over one another. That place is named 'Meter' up to this day. A signpost is erected there in memory of all those who perished.

The number of persons killed by those three persons is two to three thousand plus the property lost. One of them, however, was even bribed with a very beautiful girl in order to spare the life of the girl's father. The girl's father was one of Rumbek's most famous chiefs. Just see, a Dinka girl given free without payment of the bride price!

'Am I worse than these three?' Leo questioned himself. 'The Dinka people have forgotten their deeds. The three have lived peacefully among them. The children of the three are today regarded as good persons, despite the atrocities and havoc committed by their parents. These children were reared with the property and wealth contaminated with the blood of their own innocent people. Our Lord's saying, 'A bad tree cannot bear good fruit,' is not encompassed by Dinka norms, concepts and notions. The three have lived peacefully among them to old age, the very people who slaughtered their relatives and friends by the thousands.' Leo thought, 'Why would I not be forgiven and the people forget what I have done!!!'

CHAPTER TWENTY ONE

Leo recalled the time he left Wau with a convoy going to Raga, then to Dien in Darfur. There, he was arrested for no cause. He was found with some Fertit young men who were accused over a very small matter. He was abused and treated like a common criminal by the town's security. Leo showed his army and militia documents and his ranks in both, but they were thrown in his face. The security men even called him, *mutemerid* and *abid*. He was beaten and tortured like any other common southerner. When he was released without charge or accusation, he returned to Raga.

In Raga he had second thoughts. The very people he supported one hundred percent had classed him with other southerners, even though he was a diehard government supporter. In Wau, he used to call the Dinka and Jur *mute-meridin*, but in Dien and maybe in other parts of northern Sudan he and his compatriots were mutineers and slaves.

Leo decided to look for a job in Raga. The people he had helped were very ungrateful. He, Leo or Pio as he was known by his real name, would try to forget the havoc and atrocities he had committed. He hoped the other people would forget and forgive him. 'I have repented. That is why I left leading the militia. My hands have now become clean, unlike the three other persons. Let the Almighty forgive me. Anyhow, the Arabs and the Dinka are bad people.'

Leo would have continued in his introspection had a large herd of cattle not come hurrying between them and the bamboo grove. More and more cattle kept rushing and hurrying in large numbers till the space or distance between them and the bamboo grove was occupied by the mass of moving animals. Herdsmen ran after the cattle with whips and shouting at the top of their voices to make the cattle run faster to enter the bamboo grove.

After an hour and a half standing and sitting, the last herd entered the grove. Four young men carrying guns came hurrying and following the cattle. The sun had already set but it was relatively light, light enough to see people. The four young men had nearly passed them by when they became aware of two horses standing nearby. Kedit and Riel called to them in Dinka, 'Duok ke kat, ok aa kac kun.' The young men came back. Kedit and Riel were

told that the militias accompanying the trains were searching for cattle on both sides of the rail line. Several groups
among them had gone back to the track for the night but
one group had not returned or had not been found or seen.
They were probably spending the night nearby in order
to take the cattle early in the morning.

'We have come to give warning to the herdsmen and
the inhabitants who have escaped here, not to come out of
the bamboo grove, or to graze the cattle outside it till we
tell them to do so. We are scouts who follow the militia's
movement to and fro in their fateful journey to Wau and
back. The militia has failed to find cattle this time since
they left the river.'

Kedit asked, 'Where are the trains by now?'

One of the scouts called Awer answered, 'They are
spending the night between Alok and Udici. The trains will
enter Wau tomorrow afternoon. The militia group which
did not return to the train is desperate. They want to loot
the cattle at any cost to take to Wau for sale. It is one of
their incentives for accompanying the trains.

'We must find out where that group is spending the
night. Tomorrow is a crucial day for us. If we find them,
we shall shoot at them in order to deter them from coming
to hunt for cattle in the morning. Some of our men have
gone to engage the groups which are spending the night
near the trains.

'Tonight, you will hear the sound of heavy guns firing
all along the railway line in all directions. Our people are

to provoke the shelling till the early hours of the morning, before they leave the place. The militia fighters and the army soldiers do not leave the place where they are spending the night before sunrise. By sunrise our men would have left and be here. We shall all enter the bamboo grove.

'The bamboo grove is impenetrable to the Arabs or their horses. If they make the attempt, we shall finish killing all of them even with our spears. The Arabs would not be able to extricate themselves from the cluster of bamboos, the trees and thick grass. It is for this reason that we want the herdsmen not to allow the cattle to graze outside the bamboo grove till the enemy has entered Wau.'

Kedit asked, 'Where shall we find people in order to leave our horses and the loads they are carrying?'

Kun, another young man leading the scouts, said, 'We shall take you to them. The people are not far from where we are now.'

These young men call themselves 'scouts' a term known only to those who are educated. But to the local people, they are 'fast runners' because many of them run very fast. They track down the movement of the enemy, even those who ride on horseback. They reliably report to the people the direction of the enemy or where the enemy has gone and where they spend the night, so that the people can hide from them.

'Two of us will accompany you in search of the missing group,' Kedit offered. 'We want to put a bullet through some of them. They are the cause of our plight for all these past days. If we find them tonight or tomorrow it is either them or us. I mean the two of us here,' he said, pointing at Riel.

The scouts and the men they escorted found some elderly men sitting in a group on the grass discussing the situation their people were in. The sight of the horses nearly put them to flight. Kun had to stop them from fleeing. They recognized his voice and calm was restored. Kun told the elders where they had come upon the three persons and the two horses. 'The young men are ready to move with us tonight. They have a lot of reckoning to do with the Arab militia. The horses and this man were captured by them. The man and the horses will have to remain with you and the two young men must leave with us to search for the militia group which has not returned to spend the night near the trains with the rest of their forces.'

An elder named Kondit asked both of them to sit down on the grass and have some meat before going away. No one asked for the names of the newcomers. They were SPLA soldiers and ready to seek out the enemy. If found they would fight.

Some meat was served. The young men ate including the scouts, all except Leo who gave some lame excuse. The loads on the horses were untied and the horses were led out of the grove to graze. Someone was put in charge of the horses.

The elders were told in whispers to be very careful with Leo. He should not be allowed to escape. His behavior the previous night and by day, today had not been cordial. A man was ordered to guard Leo. The man was armed with many spears. He was told to kill Leo if he attempted to escape. He must be watched the whole night. The young men left with Kedit and Riel.

CHAPTER TWENTY TWO

The night search was in vain. The scouts found no militia spending the night elsewhere. The other fast runners went to engage the sleeping forces in order to provoke them into shelling the area but this did not materialize either. The missing militia group reached the other forces at midnight before the first bullet was fired. The scouting party was nearly engulfed by the arriving government militia. They were missed by only a few meters.

If they had shot at the sleeping forces they would have been found and annihilated. The missing militia group arrived behind them. They were talking at the top of their voices. The scouts had to squeeze themselves into a small bush. The militias were disappointed. They walked on both sides of the bush, talking and laughing till they reached their sleeping place. None of them tried to spy into the bush.

The ten-man group had to walk back to the bamboo grove. The grove was between eight and ten miles away or more. The group met Riel and Kedit with four men waiting for them. Riel and Kedit walked behind the other eight scouts. They were unhappy because they had failed to engage the militia men in a fight. The memories of what had driven them into the Fertit jungle for several days did not leave them. They wanted to avenge the ordeal they had undergone.

A mile or so away from the grove, Kedit and Riel remained sitting under the shade of the only tree standing in the place. There were no other trees or tall grass between the tree and the bamboo grove. Kedit lay down and took some hours nap. Riel remained in a sitting position, drowsy. He opened his eyes from time to time and surveyed the scene around them.

When Kedit awoke around midday he saw five horses coming towards them. The horses were a mile or so away. They were heading straight to the tree where they sat. Kedit told Riel to get ready.

'Five persons on horseback are approaching us. Lie down flat while I hide behind the tree. Take care of the two horses in front and I will take care of the rest.'

Before Kedit had finished talking the horsemen rearranged themselves. The horses stretched themselves in a line and walked abreast towards the tree.

'Now take care of the two horses to the left. I will kill the other three. Shoot at the people in the head or any fatal part, not at the horses. The horses are walking, not galloping.'

Within a few seconds, the young men blew off the heads of four riders. The fifth quickly turned his horse and almost escaped when Kedit shot at his horse from behind. The horse went down headlong and fell, instantly killing its rider

Kedit and Riel went and collected the guns and the ammunition carried by the horses' riders. Five more guns and ammunitions were added to their arms collection.

When the scouts heard the sound of gunshots, all of them ran back to the two young men, thinking that they had been attacked by the Arabs. But the scouts saw no movement of people or horses. Reaching the tree they found five dead people and a dead horse.

The four riders died sitting in their saddles, their heads hanging down loosely on the horses' sides. The horses did not escape but stood where the riders got killed. The scouts pulled down the dead riders whose feet still hung from the horses' saddles. Kedit and Riel did not touch the horses or the dead persons.

The scouts removed two keys fastened by chains round the necks of three of the corpses, all of them Arabs. The other two were Dinka men, their allies, whose job was to find out where the Dinka cattle camps could be located. After that they were to go back to Kordofan or Darfur and lead the militia men to where the cattle camps were there.

The cattle are rounded up and the Dinka men are paid in kind for their dirty work.

Every time the Murahliin left Kordofan or Darfur, the Dinka spies went ahead to find out where the cattle camps were, and also to find out whether there was an SPLA presence in the area or not. After getting the information, the Dinka men reported back to their Arab collaborators. The Dinka men had no keys found attached to their necks, only the three Arabs who were Muslims.

The scouts took the three chains with keys attached to Kedit and Riel. One key was long and looked like a cross where it was fastened to the chain. The other key was small. All were beautifully manufactured and were attached to a strong chain passed through the eye of each key. Kedit took the three chains with keys and pocketed them without giving a second thought to their use or importance.

Kedit, Riel and the scouts spent the rest of the daylight under the tree. No militia or anyone else came or was seen moving. By about sunset they all went back to where they had left the elders. Food and some meat were served. The four horses were tethered together in the place of the previous night with the two other horses. The booty collected was splendid; horses, guns and ammunitions.

But Leo was missing. Enquiring about him, one of the elders named Aterdit requested the two young men not to talk about him. He was going to relate to them and to the people there present, the atrocities and havoc Pio Ukolo meted to the people of Wau.

'The name he gave you is a false one. His real name is Pio Ukolo from Bazia. He was next to the man who headed the Fertit Militia.

'He was a trained soldier in the Sudan Army. Pio carried out several raids with his Arab masters into the Dinka and Jur quarters of the town. He was the one who instructed the Fertit youth in how to use grenades. He was the torturer and executor of all those who were arrested and innocently sentenced to be killed by the men of the military intelligence.'

CHAPTER TWENTY THREE

'I have a lot to tell you about him. He is at present answering charges brought against him in front of the creator.

'Let us rest and be ready for the militia who will be bound to come here tomorrow. The absence of their comrades, the ones you killed will prompt them to come.'

Kedit innocently pulled out the chains with the keys attached to them. He showed them to Aterdit. Aterdit laughed loudly and heartily.

'Oh dear, oh dear, you have killed Mujihadin. They are those who fight on behalf of Allah and the State. The keys are for opening the gates of rooms reserved only for the faithful as el Turabi and el Bashir preached. The longer key with something like a cross at the hilt is for heaven's main gate. The smaller and shorter one is for a suite of rooms, beautifully furnished with the best and most expensive fabrics never produced or seen in any corner of the earth. Each room in the suite is occupied by the most beautiful virgin or virgins, seventy-two of them, those that heaven provides for the pleasure of the Mujihad. Allah has promised the Mujihadin the greatest happiness in heaven, a happiness which is not granted other Muslim believers.

'However, the keys are manufactured in Allah's industrial area around Khartoum. A Mujihad must carry the keys around his neck, day and night. He must not lose them, or carelessly leave them in any place, because they can be picked up by a non-Mujihad who can avail himself of the suite reserved especially for a Mujihad and usurp his position. By carrying the keys and die fighting on behalf of Allah and the State, a person is one hundred percent sure to enter heaven. The Mujihad is taken to a special area and rooms especially reserved for them by Allah.

'However, el Bashir and el Turabi do not provide the device or means of transport for the Mujihad to ascend to heaven easily. It is stated that any Mujihad wanting to enter heaven quickly and easily must travel to John Garang de Mabior. Garang has the quickest means of dispatching the Mujihad to heaven. Whenever a Mujihad reaches Garang's territory the process to go to heaven becomes easy and simple. Garang is able to dispatch several thousand Mujihadin in less than a day to Allah's reserved residences.

'Hearing how easy and simple it was to reach Allah,

several professors, lawyers, doctors and wealthy believers availed themselves of the privilege. Most of those important, learned and wealthy persons flocked to Garang's den. They wouldn't allow the poor and simple soldiers to get the privilege first. Most of these important personalities left their universities and other important occupations and came to Garang for easy and quick transportation to Allah's suites where the beautiful virgins await them.'

Aterdit had extensive knowledge about what went on in el Bashir and el Turabi circles. Muslims believe that Allah and heaven adhere to whatever the two preached on earth. Even the keys manufactured on earth are fit to open all heaven's gates and doors. It was only necessary to put in a key made or manufactured in Khartoum and the room or rooms open. Allah does not reject a Mujihad dispatched by el Bashir and el Turabi even if that person has a lot of blood on his hands.

Aterdit continued, 'As for the man you brought and who gave you a false name, he is no longer here. He has gone to his creator like the Mujihad you killed. When I saw him, I could not control myself. I had no stomach to contain and reflect on his past deeds. I had promised to kill him as soon as I set my eyes on him and whenever I found him. You are free to accuse me to any higher authorities. I cannot regret taking the life of that stooge. If the next chance avails itself, I will also get rid of the head, for it is the tail that I have severed. I will be happy if chance gives me their leader.

'My boys, forget about Pio and be prepared for the militia and the Mujihadin who will surely come tomorrow. It is evening now. The Mujihadin and the militia men are not permitted to spend the night far from the main body or far from the trains. They will surely come in search of their missing comrades.

'You killed three Mujihadin. The other two were from our own people, hired to show the enemy where the cattle camps are and where people have gone to. To el Bashir and El Turabi, the Dinka renegades get their reward here on earth in the form of cattle. They are not entitled to a place in heaven. Heaven is reserved only for Muslims and nobody else.'

CHAPTER TWENTY FOUR

arly next morning and up to midday no Mujihad or
militia man appeared. The cattle grazed inside the
bamboo grove for most of the day. Towards evening
some cattle got out of the grove to graze. They were not
forced back.

The two young men and the so-called scouts sat in front
of the bamboo grove waiting to repulse the attackers. If
they could not, then they would enter the grove like the
other unarmed citizens. By early evening the scouts were
nonplussed and left in search for the Mujihadin and their
allies the militia men. What had happened? On the way
they met two persons coming back from Udici. The two
reported that the trains had already arrived in Wau. The
commander of the convoy left very early in the morning

and allowed no men to remain behind, be they Mujihadin or militia men. No good or bad reason was given or heard. Why such a hurry? Maybe tomorrow something will be heard.

The scouts went back before sunset. They reported what they had heard from the two persons returning from Udici. Udici was a police station with a few soldiers and policemen, most of them Arabs and Fertit. However, some Jur and Dinka local people used to go to Udici daily. The soldiers and policemen would not harass or arrest them.

They were the source of information about the presence of SPLA forces in the area, either in great numbers or whether they have an intention to attack the station or not. Sometimes they even allowed some SPLA soldiers to come and spend daytime hours in the station. It was a way of maintaining peace between them and the local SPLA forces stationed in the area.

After taking some food and milk, Aterdit called the two young soldiers, Kedit and Riel with the scouts and related to them a tale about Pio Ukolo, who renamed himself Leo.

He said 'Pio Ukolo was one of the founders of the Fertit militia and a leading member. He was a trained soldier in the government army. When the Fertit intended to form a militia against the movement, but which later turned out to be against Jur and Dinka people, he was requested to train the youth and anybody eligible to carry arms. It was at first voluntary but later it became compulsory for the whole Fertit community, including women.

'After training a few youths, he instructed them to destroy some Dinka and Jur businesses in the villages outside Bussere. He wanted to test how the Regional Government in Wau would react to their action. There was a police station in Bussere and an army unit guarding Bussere bridge. There were some Dinka and Jur men in arms in those units.

'But Pio had backing in army circles. The army commander in Girinti gave him the go ahead. Before the destruction of those businesses and the killing of their owners, the Dinka and Jur men in both units were brought back to Wau.

'The Arabs and the Fertit soldiers and policemen were the only people left. The Dinka and Jur people living in Bussere failed to grasp what was going on around them. They were aware of the militia and a few lynchings they carried out against some members of their communities residing in the Fertit villages.

'One evening a Fertit woman married to a Dinka man was passing near a house where Pio and the youth were planning an attack. She overheard her husband's name, the position of their home, shop and those who were to be lynched and the shops to be destroyed.

'Pio who came from Khartoum was to launch the attack followed by those from Wau whose names Kon's wife did not know. Kon, the Fertit woman's husband was well known to people living in Bussere. Most residents of Bussere regarded him as their brother-in-law and friend.

Almost all of them shied away from attacking him and destroying his property.

'Pio took it upon himself to carry out the attack with all those who did not know Kon. The planned attack was to take place at midnight, after the Dinka and the Jur were in bed. Then they were to be ordered to come out of the huts one by one and be killed. Those who refused were to be burned alive in their huts if the huts contained no valuable furniture or useful things.

'But Kon's house was to be spared. He was to be killed but his property was to be reserved for the militia's activities. His house was to be used as offices and the compound turned into a training ground.

'Kon's wife couldn't bear to hear the rest. She ran home and dispatched their young son to go and urgently call his father. Before the child could reach his father, the woman ran to the shopping center. She thought her husband would not respond quickly to her call. The man's life was in danger. The time was already after nine o'clock. Midnight was not far away.

'The woman met Kon on the way. He wanted to go and take something from the house. Bussere market used to close after ten o'clock. Kon was going to bring something he forgot to the shop for the following day. The woman stopped her husband and pulled him out of the path and away from anyone's hearing. She related to her husband the plan and how it was to be executed by midnight.

'She ordered her husband to go back. "Take away any

cash in the shop and leave at once. Take nothing that could be seen. Tell your friend Ucu the Jur man and the two of you must be off before ten o'clock. I shall try to save myself and the children. My brothers will help me to hide till tomorrow. Tell no one otherwise all of you will be rounded up and killed before the set time comes. Do not follow the road or any path. Walk through the grass to safety."

'Without a word Kon hurried back to the market, to where he kept his money. He opened the box and pocketed the cash. He went to Ucu's shop. He whispered to him and went back to close his shop. Ucu stood stunned. He tried to think about what to do. He even failed to take all the money he had.

'Kon closed his shop as usual and went back to Ucu. He told Ucu in a loud voice that they were to dine in his house tonight. His wife had prepared a special meal for them. Ucu should not go to eat in the restaurant. Ucu still doubted what Kon told him so he closed his shop slowly still trying to process what Kon told him.

'By the time the shops closed and they were about to leave the market center, several youths appeared from several directions carrying guns. The youth pretended to check how secure the shops were. That used to be the work of the police. Why youth today? This sent a clear message to Ucu. Something nasty was in the air.

'Kon and Ucu took the path going to Kon's home which was about half a kilometer away. The path went through a patch of tall thick grass. It was in the month of August.

Although they were taller than the grass the darkness of the night covered them.

'Halfway they met Kon's wife coming running. She caught her husband's hands weeping. "What are you still doing here and why are you going back to the house? Some Dinka and Jur people are already rounded up and are being slaughtered. Jump into the grass. Go and die where I shall not see your corpse or bones."

'The woman turned and ran back. She found many militia youth in her compound most of them from Wau. She was prevented from entering her house. The woman had already removed most of her valuables and her children were taken away by her relatives.

'Kon and Ucu disappeared behind some thick bush several meters from the shopping center and his home. Many bushes stood midway between the path going to Kon's house and the road going to Wau. A lot of commotion and cries reached where the two were hiding. Kon even heard the lamentations of his wife. She was being beaten and questioned about the whereabouts of her husband before she was hacked to death.

'Several people ran here and there. Children and women were crying seeing their fathers and husbands being chopped with machetes and pangas. All the Dinka and Jur shops were looted and set ablaze. Kon and Ucu could see several youth, men and Fertit standing and dancing in the market. The burning shops lit up the whole place and everything and everybody could be seen dancing happily in groups.

'Kon and Ucu remained hidden till late midnight. The two found their way through the dew-covered grass to Bussere bridge. Soldiers were camped on both sides of the bridge to guard it, but no sentinels stood guard at the entry to the bridge at night. The nearest tukul to the bridge was ten or more meters away and on both sides. The river was getting full. Kon could swim across it but Ucu could not cover half the distance. The soldiers were all fast asleep and the two men tip toed to the bridge and left it on the other side in the same manner.

'They were lucky. After a few moments some Dinka young men came running, trying to escape from the youth who chased them with guns. They wanted to cross to safety across the bridge. But the soldiers heard sounds of yelling and calling, *mutemeridin, mutemeridin*. The escapees were rounded up and handed back to the pursuers.

'The young people were not taken far. They were chopped to pieces with machetes and dumped into a ditch a few meters away from the main road and about a hundred meters from the bridge. The soldiers who handed over those unfortunate victims, hailed and congratulated the young Fertit militia. They had begun to teach the Dinka and the Jur a lesson they would never forget.

'That was the first act of your man who renamed himself Leo Richard. Indeed, he has been absent from Wau for some years now.

'When no response came from the authorities in Wau about the death and plight of the Dinka and Jur people,

Pio moved to Wau. He stayed near Agok Leprosy Hospital with members of the militia. One day, four young Dinka boys from Twic visited one of their relatives admitted to the hospital. The Fertit and the Arab soldiers guarding the hospital sent word to the militia – *laham, laham.*

'The militia understood the call – *meat, meat.* It meant a Jur or a Dinka to be killed. The militia under the command of Pio went to the path between Wau and Agok Hospital and waited for the four boys. The four were intercepted on the road and murdered a few meters away from the road. Their dead bodies were dumped into a ditch close by.

'When news about the missing boys reached the sick man, he left his hospital bed. He wanted to go and ascertain what had happened to the missing boys from relatives in Wau. He also fell into the hands of the militia which had set up a permanent presence along the road to intercept those going or leaving the hospital. The sick man was also killed and his dead body thrown into the ditch where the corpses of the four boys were rotting. The corpses of these persons were found by a person going by car to visit the sick man who had been hospitalized.

'Pio carried out several night raids into Dinka and Jur quarters at Nazareth and elsewhere. He also instructed the Fertit youth in the use of grenades. Almost every night grenades exploded in the homes of Dinka and Jur people, maiming and killing several persons including women, children and old aged.

'The use of grenades stopped when a desperate and

gallant Dinka youth threw a grenade into the house of some Arab traders. Several Arab traders nighty gathered in the house and feasted there. Many of them were boozing and others played cards. The grenade killed several of them and wounded a score.

'Pio was hailed a hero in Fertit circles, especially during the time of Abu Gurun Abdalla Abu Gurun. Abu Gurun permitted Pio and the militia to kill the Dinka and the Jur at will. No one was to question him or the deeds committed by the militia.

'As a military commander of Bahr el Ghazal military area, Abu Gurun was the law. He had sanctioned the deeds of the Fertit militia. The Dinka and Jur with their other allies were rebels at heart even if they did not join the movement. They formed a fifth column, an enemy living among the innocent Fertit. Their tribesmen, women and children had engineered the rebellion against the Sudan Government. To get rid of them was permissible.

'Pio recruited every able-bodied Fertit into the militia and that included the members of the other organized forces and civilians. Every Fertit had to enlist in the militia. All those drafted were given ranks according to the number of enemy persons they had killed. Any Fertit who was not a member of the militia was regarded as an enemy of the people.'

Aterdit would have continued had the scouts and the young soldiers not requested him to allow them to rest. They would listen to his tale the following day. Aterdit was a talkative person with a vast knowledge of the affairs of the Sudan. He was enlightened about everything that had happened since the Torit uprising.

CHAPTER TWENTY FIVE

The following morning three members of the scouting team went to Udici. One of them was known to most of the soldiers and the policemen. He was informed that three or four days ago the Arab tribes of Darfur and those of Kordofan had fought a bitter pitched battle back home. Fighters lost their lives on both sides. The loss of life was said to be very great.

News of the fight reached Wau from government and military sources.

The commander of the convoy was requested to separate the Mujihadin and the militia men according to their regions, Darfur and Kordofan. The men from Darfur were to walk on the western side of the railway line and the trains, while those from Kordofan were to move to the eastern side of the line.

The five trains and government soldiers were to walk between the two groups forming a buffer zone. The two groups were separated by a distance of a kilometer on either side. The two groups were not allowed to have any contact whatsoever.

Reaching Wau the people of Kordofan were left to stay near the trains. Those from Darfur were accommodated near Wau airstrip. A heavy security force was posted between them night and day.

Next morning the government started to airlift the people of Darfur to Nyala. There were four flights daily till the last Mujihad or militia man was transported back to Darfur. Those from Kordofan were to use the trains to go back. The trains were being off loaded quickly in order to let them leave Wau. None of the warring tribesmen were allowed to enter the town of Wau or leave the place of their accommodation.

The government and military authorities did not want the news to reach the ears of the people from those places. Strict orders were issued to the soldiers moving between them not to disclose the news. However, the Mujihadin and the militia men suspected that something bad must have occurred behind them at home. All knew that they always fight among themselves as tribes but not Darfur versus Kordofan.

The trains transported the people of Kordofan back to Muglad. They did not stop on the way back unless attacked by the SPLA. The trains left Wau very early in the morning to reach Aweil before sunset. The following day, they would be at Bahr el Arab railway station. There, the trains would be in Kordofan area where any Mujihad or militia man would be free to go to their various areas. The Mujihadin and militia men would be given money for their transport if they had no horses. Those with horses would use them. The horses belonging to the people of Darfur were to be sold and their proceeds sent after them.

The two young men remained the whole week waiting for the trains to pass. They wanted to see a train for they had not seen one before. The rains had become less and less heavy. Some elderly citizens went back to their villages, but the young men and girls had remained behind with the cows. There was plenty of milk because here plenty of grass for cattle was available.

At the beginning of the second week, the trains passed unannounced. The scouts returned with the news that the trains had reached Aweil two days previous. The scouts told the cattle-rearers to leave for the villages. It was cultivation time and the people at home needed milk to feed on. There was no longer any need to fear. The enemy had retreated till the next dry season.

Kedit and Riel wanted to leave at once and make for their unit's headquarters, but the scouts would not permit them to do so. They were to go first to the village where their *Banybith* resides. He had sent a message to that effect. 'The two young men must appear before me, before going to where they came from.' The man of Nhialic wanted to see, the two of them in person before they returned to their unit.

Kedit and Riel arrived at the village of the Banybith. The man of Nhialic would not talk to them till two days had passed. He had rites to perform. The young men were brought before him after two days stay in the village. The leader of the scouts had to entertain the two in his home. The young men spent a very happy two days feasting, and dances were performed in their honor.

On the third day they were taken before the man of Nhialic. He talked to them a lot enquiring about their places of origin and families. He then said,

Nhialic wa, kony ee mithke. Ace weng duntok kene kony. Kony kek wada, bik a bak te koric. Nyin maac ace lony ke guop. Nhialic wa, gaam ha thok. Kek aa dhiop bik hen wuor. Nhialic wei weng, ku raan kek aye ku kek long.

The old man then sprayed them with much water. He poured the small amount of water which remained in the calabash on their feet. He told them to leave his compound and not to look behind till they had reached the place where they were accommodated. After that the old man instructed one of his sons to accompany the two to their unit's headquarters. Kedit and Riel left four horses and five AK47 guns captured near the bamboo grove at the disposal of the man of Nhialic.

After two days walk Kedit and Riel arrived at their last destination. The son of Banybith gave each of them a small spear. He told each of them not to part with the spear when going into combat. They were gifts from his father. Then he left.

Kedit and Riel remained at the unit headquarters. They presented the two horses with the loads of guns and ammunition to the area commander. Later they had to relate to the officers and men of their unit, the ordeal of their plight.

Lino Angok Kuec
Kuajok
December 2013

THE FIRST DAY
OF THE COMPREHENSIVE
PEACE AGREEMENT (C.P.A.)

CHAPTER ONE

It was the first day the soldiers heard no news or rumors of an imminent or pending attack. As usual most of them woke early. All had packed and tied up most of their personal belongings, battle equipment and even arms and ammunition. All that the soldiers were accustomed to do was done and they were just as alert. A few soldiers were cleaning their personal guns or greasing them or assembling the guns' accessories. Some soldiers stood chanting in a group or singing war songs.

Suddenly it dawned on them – peace had come. The soldiers did not know how to react. That first day became the opposite of every day of the last twenty-two years. It was early in the morning and the soldiers were already bored. What were they to do? What were they to talk about? Where were they to go?

The talk was usually about how to repulse an impending enemy attack, which place to go or where to render support to hard pressed units. The soldiers were always on the move, carrying their personal sleeping things, guns, extra ammunition and other heavy guns. They ate whatever came their way or what was offered them. In most cases the soldiers went hungry for several days on end or had plenty to eat when chance supplied it. What the soldiers were accustomed to was eating by chance, not to their desired taste or eating to the full. Today, after several days fasting, hunger began to pinch each of them. Hunger is not easily felt when one is on the move or when there is looming tension in the air or real tension.

Today, they were to test the Dinka saying *yac aa adung Nhialic*. Is the stomach really the calabash of God? When the soldiers are on the move coming across villages, they come upon something to eat. On this first day of peace nobody moved and nothing was expected to come. The village that peace found this unit in was a very small one.

The officer in charge of the unit realized how bored his

soldiers were on that first day of the peace agreement and the cease fire. If he left them thus the soldiers might escape to nearby villages and try to get something to eat, even by force from the already disheartened local population. So, Captain Limlim called the whole unit together around him. He ordered the soldiers to sit around and pay attention to what he was going to tell them. Captain Limlim said, 'Today is a special day in all these years. Never did we sit and have friendly conversation. Today and the days coming we are to rest. Try to forget and put behind all that you had accustomed yourselves to during the war, good or bad. Let us think and talk about our immediate pending problems. Can any of you tell us one thing the peace agreement and cease fire cannot give us today and which bothers us at this particular moment?'

Lual Yai, a talkative soldier, raised his hand and said, 'The constant carrying of weapons and ammunition.'

'No,' replied the officer. 'We may not continue for long to carry them on our heads and shoulders. The movement may provide the means of transport to take us and our weaponry to where it is to be located for us or to our brigade.'

Ador, another soldier put in, 'The filthy clothes we have on, walking bare foot and going without pay.'

'No again,' replied Limlim. 'Don't think about things of tomorrow, a week or a month from now. Think of what is dogging us today. The other things are general for the whole of the whole SPLA. Think about us as a unit and only for today.'

A young soldier named Noon Dut shouted from behind the officer and said, 'Sir, it is hunger. I am now as hungry as a dog.'

'That's it,' Captain Limlim confirmed. 'I think all of us are as hungry as Noon. It is not you alone Noon. No one has eaten a morsel of food since yesterday morning. Hunger still menaces us. I fear we may not have anything nice and enough to eat as usual. My last square meal was two days ago. Yesterday I ate only boiled sorghum mixed with some maize. We were many and I think each one of us had only two or three mouthfuls.'

Ador added, 'I am in a worse state than you sir. My last big meal was three days ago. Although I gorged myself to the brim with that bad food, nothing has come my way for the last two days. Not even boiled sorghum which you ate. However, our people say, *yac aaduok Nhalic* – God always takes care of it.'

Captain Limlim answered, 'Don't be a fool Ador. Here under this tree will something to munch ever come to us of its own accord? It was the bellies of the children of Israel which God filled with manna. They didn't work for it, but their duty was to collect it where it fell. We must search for food, but where shall we go to? The local population is no longer going to support us. The war is over and the movement has not taken up the reins of power in the towns where there is money to purchase food for the army, and not for us alone but for all the SPLA.'

Ador said again, 'I still insist sir, *yac aaduok Nhalic*. Our people believe it and so do I…'

Before Ador could complete his sentence, the unit saw two soldiers pulling a huge fat ox. The soldiers used two ropes to pull the ox. All the soldiers turned their attention to the two men leading and struggling with the ox to where the soldiers sat. No one spoke but continued to gaze at the two soldiers and the ox. Lual Yai became impatient. He shouted to the two soldiers struggling with the ox, 'Where are you taking the ox?'

The two soldiers replied in unison, 'Come and help us. The ox is for you people. The commanding officer has sent it to you.'

All the soldiers laughed at once. Many of them congratulated Ador and said, 'Really *yac aaduok Nhalic*. We did not expect to get something so soon to feed on today.'

Furthermore, the two soldiers informed the officer that his unit was to remain where it was. He would receive further instructions where to station the whole brigade. Some food would be sent to them starting from next week.

In a few moments the ox was slaughtered, skinned and its meat was roasted on a big fire. When the cooked meat was ready, it was spread on clean leaves. The unit sat around the burnt meat and ate. While eating, the soldiers began to crack jokes. As soon as the burned meat was consumed, the cooks went to cook part of the meat for the evening meal. A portion was left for the following morning.

After eating the meat and resting awhile, the officer again called all the soldiers together to be near him under the tree. They continued with their conversation. The officer did not want any of the soldiers to escape or to go elsewhere that day. He wanted to engage the soldiers so that they did not leave the compound. The officer knew that when soldiers are idle, they cause trouble to themselves and to other citizens.

Captain Limlim began again.

'Many of you here come from different squads, platoons, companies and even battalions. Some come from units outside the region. Each of you might have undergone tough and dangerous missions. Can any of you relate to us any such dire undertakings?'

Several soldiers raised their hands. Each of them wanted to relate the circumstances he and his unit endured. A quiet, composed and respected corporal known as Abu-Naar, so nicknamed because of his bravery and talent on the field of battle, was chosen by captain Limlim.

Abu-Naar stated that he came from Blood Battalion. He said he was once ordered out from the training center with a platoon of soldiers he was in charge of. He headed for Kiirkou in Twic area from somewhere in Tonj. All his men including himself did not know the route to follow.

'We were ordered to take some ammunition to a company that was hard pressed by the enemy. The unit was running out of ammunition. It was mid to late March. It was damn hot and the sun was fierce. There were no people living in the villages enroute to Kiirkou especially around Gogrial.

'It was the time Kerubino's forces had terrorized and devastated the whole of Twic, Awan Mou and Aguok. Most of the villages in these areas were deserted. There was no water to be found anywhere, let alone anything to eat. We were heavily loaded and crushed by the weight we bore.

'We carried three or four AK47 rifles each plus a box containing 500 rounds of ammunition, and five magazines were strapped to our chests. The load was excessive and extremely heavy. We covered not more than four or five miles per day.

'On very rare occasions we came across someone who could help us with the load. They could not be persuaded to help so we had to use force to get them to carry a box containing ammunition. But when we were near river Jur near Gogrial town finding people to help us became difficult or almost impossible. No people lived in the villages we passed through. We covered a distance of ten miles in three days. The food we had was gone four days before reaching the river.

By the time we arrived at Agor (that is river Jur) between Gogrial and Panacier, we were spent. Hunger, fatigue and thirst had taken their toll. The river was dry. We had to dig in the sand in the riverbed to get some drinking water. We drank but our stomachs were empty and the water gurgled inside us. Some of us nearly vomited out the water. We lay down to rest and set a guard to stand and keep watch for one hour only. He had to be very vigilant. We all kept guard for one hour including myself.

'We imagined that the nearest village was at least five to ten miles away. We expected no people to be in it. Kerubino's Nyigat had terrorized and devastated the whole area and had driven away the inhabitants of those villages near Gogrial town. The place was deathly quiet and calm. One of us named Alueth (God have mercy and rest his soul in peace) got up and walked slowly along the riverbank. No one knew where he was going. He could not have been going for a call of nature because our stomachs had been empty for the last seventy-two hours. However, he walked away along the riverbank and the guard followed him with his eyes. We were all lying down but not asleep, awake and extremely hungry.

'Suddenly Alueth waved his arm and turned back limping. The guard shouted, 'Get up and take positions.' We got up hurriedly ready to face whatever Alueth had seen. We ran and took up positions from the few trees near our resting place. Then Aluet realized his mistake. He signaled to us not to panic, but we remained standing motionless, ready to repulse whatever was coming behind him. Between Gogrial and Panacier was a no man's land where the Nyigat of Kerubino moved at will. Kerubino's forces had driven away the local inhabitants. At first we thought that Alueth had spotted Nyigat, but now Alueth's second signal allayed our anxiety and we no longer feared an enemy attack.

'When Alueth reached us, he told us to calm down and go back and sit on our plastic sheets. "You can't imagine or believe what I'm going to tell you. It is something unimaginable and impossible to be seen or found in this dry parched river."

'Now *Alueth* almost matched his name. He was prone to lying without shame or fear. He would say something that frightened the hearers even if it was small and simple, and so many of us shouted at him, "Alueth! Stop your lies and exhortation! Tell us what you have found or seen. This is not the place or time to lie or to deceive or joke with people as you usually do."

"I am not lying, joking or deceiving. Collect a lot of firewood. You are going to feast on the meat of one of the biggest animals the river contains," said Alueth.

"Alueth, you are already lying and being deceitful. Which animal can live in this dry, parched river? A crocodile buries itself in a dry hole by this stage of the season. It cannot be found in a dry riverbed as this is by now. As for a hippo, it always stays where there is water, not on dry land or in a dry riverbed such as this."

"I am telling the truth, *A nak Nhialic hen*," protested Alueth.

"Then tell us. What have you found or seen?"

"There's a huge hippo lying in very shallow water down there where I went. The shallow water is inside the riverbank, dug deep inside the bank by the flowing current. Most of its body is outside the water. However, the shadow of the riverbank covers it. Let your most accurate marksman follow me. If he doesn't find the hippo, let him shoot me dead instead of the animal and not come back to you for orders."

'We were surprised by his talk and gave him a warning. "Alueth, a hungry person can act ruthlessly. Don't mess with us. We shall leave your carcass here for the birds of prey to feast on." But Alueth just laughed.

'Our most accurate marksman went to where Alueth said he saw the hippo, and I instructed him not to reflect or hesitate. "Either you kill the hippo or Alueth goes to the next world never to lie again. There will be no more orders This is not the time or place to lie or joke." And so we remained standing, our eyes and attention focused on the backs of the two as they walked away from us towards the unseen animal.

'A hippo generally leaves its den or herd when it's chased away from the females by a younger, stronger and more powerful male. If a hippo was there, as claimed by Alueth, then it must be a male which has escaped being killed by another stronger male. If the hippo was there, it had probably migrated here in search of safety in a different river.

'When a female hippo gives birth, she does so in secrecy. The mother first inspects the baby to see whether it's a male or female. If it's a male, she hides it from the father. If that is not possible, she migrates to a lonely place to rear her baby until the young sibling is able to defend itself or escape from its father's wrath when attacked.

'While these thoughts were passing through *my* mind, I

didn't know what the others were thinking. Suddenly we heard the burst of an AK47, and Alueth signaled to us to send more soldiers. Our marksman had approached very close to the animal and fired at its head at short range. The hippo died instantly.

'I divided the force into three groups. One was to go and skin the animal and carry the meat to where we were. It was the only place with several bushes and shady shrubs. A second group was to collect firewood and set fire to it, making ready for us to roast the meat. The third was to guard the two places. We were afraid that the enemy in Gogrial might see smoke and come to attack us and take our meat by force. Nyigat roamed the area as they pleased.

'In no time our meat was roasting on the fire and a pot full was boiling. Some of us sat around the meat and began to slice it. We placed most of the sliced meat on sedabs to dry and to smoke it when the sun went down. We did not want Nyigat to see the smoke rising from our campsite. We feasted on the burnt meat now while the meat to be smoked on the sedab would be eaten on the way to Kiirkou.

'We spent three days feasting in that place. We gave the place a name – Good and Lucky. When we left our load was heavier and we believed in the adage of our people – *yac aaduok Nhalic* – the same thing which took place today.

'However, before we left, we noticed something very strange. No birds of prey. The kites and vultures which are mostly found everywhere in the villages and in great numbers were nowhere to be seen. We left the animal's stomach, intestines, the head and the skin on the sand where the animal was butchered. We thought birds would come for these parts left in the open, but none appeared. Howbeit the first hyena arrived before sunset.

I think the hyena did not expect to find people there. The hippo had remained in the place where water was available. The hyenas and other animals drank from the waterhole when the hippo left it to graze. Several hyenas arrived after that. Many of them had cubs following. Firstly, all rushed to drink then turned to feed on the parts of the animal we had left near the water.

'The hyenas began to fight and rob each other of the parts we had left. After finishing those parts, they rushed towards us, and nearly robbed us. There were several hundred of them. The cubs were the worst. They had no fear. They were not deterred by their mothers nor by us. We increased the number of guards from the two or three chosen to watch over the meat. The hyenas were so numerous that we made a circle around the portion not put on the sedab.

'We threw bones with lots of meat on them to the kittens which had no fear of approaching us. Instead of letting the kittens eat first, the male hyenas snatched the bones and ran away with them. At times the mothers allowed the cubs to help themselves to what we threw to them but the males had no mercy. They snatched everything and ran far away to eat.

'After sunset we put a lot of firewood under the sedabs with the sliced meat on, because we were confident that the smoke could not be seen at night. The poles of the sedab we erected were tall, so tall that the hyenas' cubs could not reach the meat. The big hyenas were afraid to come near us. Many of us kept guard. We did two hours each. In the morning all vanished, but still no birds of prey came. We wondered why there were no birds in the vicinity. All that we could do was guess the cause or the reason why.

'Gogrial town, we learned later, was not far from where we were. Kerubino's forces or Nyigat resided there. They slaughtered several oxen, bulls, goats and sheep daily. It was reported that each soldier killed almost daily a male goat for himself alone, while those with wives and children slaughtered an ox for their daily needs. One to two hundred animals died every day. For that reason, all the kites, vultures and other birds which feed on animal flesh migrated to the vicinity of Gogrial up to the place where we killed the hippo. Food for the birds was plentiful and also several big and tall trees stood in the town where the birds were able to make their nests to roost, lay their eggs and hatch them.

'The Sudan Government Army soldiers also feasted on meat on a daily basis. The soldiers slaughtered the cattle at will. The Nyigat never ran short of what to kill and offer to their neighbors, the government soldiers. Entire cattle camps were rounded up and driven to Gogrial in the same manner that the Arab militia and the Murahliin did.

'Almost all the villages around Gogrial up to a distance of twenty miles or more were deserted. Kerubino's Nyigat had looted them and destroyed most of them. Some villages were burned to ashes. Kerubino's forces behaved worse than the Arabs even though they were children and citizens of Gogrial. I expected the same thing to have taken place around Wunrok where we were heading to.

'Each week Kerubino's Nyigat expanded their sphere of influence and operated further and further afield. Their usual method was to go out on looting safaris to terrorize and capture young men. The young men taken from the villages and cattle camps were well treated, re-oriented and co-opted into the militia. Finding plenty to eat and given permission to act freely, these young men readily succumbed to the credo of the GATRY forces (Gogrial, Aweil, Tonj, Rumbek and Yirol). Most of these forces were from Twic, followed by the two from Aguok.

'After spending three days in the place near the dry river, we moved out and walked at night. There was no water to be found anywhere. On the second night we bumped into a man or should I say he bumped into us. The night was dark and the thick dark forest in which we were travelling was dark. The man was going to Abiei. He almost ran away after seeing us seated in the only open space available in the middle of the forest. We ordered him not to run away or else he would be fired at. Finding that we were not Nyigat he was relieved and he calmed down. He told us that he was going to Abiei. He was walking at night in order to avoid the heat of the scorching sun and succumbing to thirst and so that he wouldn't be captured by Nyigat. One of his wives had gone to Abiei during the famine of 1986-88. He left the woman there with some children and returned to his young wife in Apuok area. The woman had refused to go to Abiei. She could manage to care for her small children. I can't remember the man's name but he became very useful to us.

'We offered him some meat. He was hungry, like anyone in the area. When he finished eating what we offered him he led us to where we could find enough water and where to spend the daytime hiding. The Nyigat regularly combed the area including this forest. The Nyigat in Wunrok and Gogrial sometimes meet in Riau searching for cattle camps and young men to boost the numbers of their army. The Nyigat had also devastated almost the whole of Twic even up to Riau, south of Lol River.

'In the evening at about eight o'clock, when it was relatively dark, our man guided us to Lol River. We crossed the river and he left us to contact our comrades. A few soldiers with a few rounds of ammunition commonly carried out reconnaissance at some distance from where Kerubino's forces deployed their men at night.

'Our newly acquired guide turned out to be an ardent supporter of the movement. He left us in a safe and secure place and went to where SPLA reconnaissance was to be found. He found them and guided them back to where he had left us. We had given him a secret password for the night. Coming close to us he uttered the word. We answered back and they approached us. The reconnaissance unit was under the command of an officer with the rank of a captain.

'The soldiers were very happy to see us and to receive some supplies. The units in the area had almost run out of bullets. The soldiers began to pick up the boxes of ammunition and the guns we carried. We asked them to sit down and have some meat. We had divided ourselves into three groups when our guide left. We asked the other two groups to join us. The meat and more boxes of ammunition were brought in. We offered food to the soldiers. Some of them might have not eaten since morning. The food boosted their morale even more. After finishing eating what was in front of them the soldiers picked up our loads, and we were left with nothing to carry except our personal guns. All that we had was taken and carried by the men of the reconnaissance.

'After we had walked for about fifteen miles to the north of Wunrok, our guide was allowed to proceed on his journey to Abiei. We thanked him heartily and wished him safe journey. I hope I shall find him during peacetime to pay back his kindness. Without his local knowledge the probability of Nyigat finding us was high. They could have killed us. If we resisted and did not surrender (and that's what we would have done), they would have killed us. We were prepared to fight to the last man.

'The forest in which the man found us was very thick

and dense. It was said to contain maneaters, leopards and hyenas. We met several hyenas while we were walking and where we spent the daytime hours waiting for sunset.

Toward evening several hyenas appeared hurrying and heading to a pond, the only one in the forest which contained water. We were heading in the same direction. The next water point was to be found in Lol River, ten to fifteen miles ahead of us. It was our guide who alone went stealthily to the pond with a jerrycan. We used the water he brought back economically to last us till the evening of that day. The forest was very quiet. All the small birds and the large ones went near the water pond. The bees did as well.

'The land and the forest were parched and dry. All that we carried remained tied together, ready to pick up and hurry away with in case of an emergency. Kerubino's Nyigat roamed the whole area freely. It was they who could move at will. SPLA forces could not. When our soldiers ran away instead of facing the enemy due to a lack of ammunition, the Nyigat accused us of cowardice.

'All the villages near and some distance away from Wunrok were also deserted. The people and cattle were moved to where the citizens thought they were out of reach of the Nyigat. However, there was no place or area anywhere in Gogrial which was out of bounds for Kerubino's Nyigat, especially when they ran out of food.

'Twic, Akuar and Kuac Payams were the worst hit. These areas were every now and then attacked by Kerubino's

Nyigat from Wunrok, Nuer Nyigat and the Murahliim. A month or two did not go by without one of the three attacking.

'Kerubino's Nyigat behaved as if they were not children of the people of this place. They looted and killed people at will. GATRY soldiers had no remorse. They looted cattle camps, raped the women and mistreated the children and old people. Some of them even killed some old people who tried to caution them. They had no respect for anybody, old or young, woman or man. Whatever Kerubino told them was the only commandment they obeyed.'

Among the soldiers listening to this story were four to ten former soldiers of GATRY. They kept their lips sealed as the others turned to glare at them with disdain, then laughed or gurgled with disappointment or disapproval. The former GATRY soldiers though showed no sign in their faces or movement. Nobody could tell whether they were sorry to hear about their past deeds or angry for whatever falsehood had been heaped upon them.

'Some GATRY Nyigat (present or absent) did very nasty things. They knew what they were doing was wrong but the reasonable ones had no power or way to prevent the others from carrying out those atrocities. The officers let the soldiers do whatever they desired without restraint or rebuke. It was their way of retaining their loyalty.

'When GATRY Soldiers were on safari raids to cattle camps or villages, each soldier acted as he desired. The goats and sheep rounded up were slaughtered mercilessly.

Each soldier killed a goat or sheep for himself, while the cattle were driven to Gogrial or Wunrok as booty for general distribution. The heads of the goats and sheep slaughtered were used as mounds to put the cooking pots on. The soldiers had no time or reason to search for earthen mounds usually used by the women.

'The meat that could not be consumed was left to the dogs, the birds of prey and the hyenas. Now the hyenas no longer looked for dogs and dogs no longer feared the hyena. It was said that the hyena and the dog had made a truce and reconciled. Plenty of meat was available for all in most areas. There was no reason for the hyenas to run after the dogs or for the dogs to take risks barking at the hyenas. A hyena only had to walk to Gogrial or Wunrok. There, plenty of meat and bones were available for no risk. Every night, meat that wasn't consumed that day was thrown outside the deployment area for the hyenas and even foxes and the birds of prey to help themselves to. The dogs ate enough inside the deployment area and in the houses of their masters.'

The soldiers talked thus, while their meat was boiling on the fire. Several pots containing meat were on the fire boiling for the afternoon and evening meals. The soup was to be drunk or used as broth. The headman of the village nearby had offered the unit a basket full of dura to grind into flour for the soldiers to eat.

As the soldiers had had enough to eat, the officer in charge wanted them to rest. Other instructions would be received later or during the coming days. The commanders at the regional headquarters tried to make sure that the soldiers remained where the peace agreement and ceasefire found them. However, the troops should remain ready to move, once ordered to do so, in case the enemy was not content with the peace deal or if the ceasefire was not respected by the other side. Arabs are unpredictable. They do not respect what they have said or stick to the terms agreed. To some of them the agreement was a sell-out. All that the South wanted was granted to them. Even self-determination which the northern politicians of the past would not hear of, was now a concrete pillar of the CPA peace agreement.

CHAPTER TWO

Before sunset, an elderly man walked into the army's camp. Behind him were several women and girls, loaded with calabashes, gourds and jerrycans. A young man carried *kou*, that is back bone meat – all for the unit present in the small village on the first day of peace.

A wedding feast was in progress in an adjacent village two miles away. The marriage guests came from Captain Limlim's area. The guests did not know that one of their sons was the commander of the unit.

It was late afternoon when the wedding guests learned about Limlim's presence in the nearby village. Besides being from their area, Limlim was a very close friend of the bridegroom. Limlim had released five cows to his friend for the marriage settlement of the bride price. Wedding guests brought with them sixty-one cows as part of the bride price payment.

When no soldier appeared as expected in the morning the wedding guests began to ask why the *kou*, meat meant for the army, had not been taken. *Kou* was that part of the cattle carcass always reserved for the soldiers, either for the wedding or as an offering to the spirits. A calabash of asida, a gourd of asilia or marisa, plus a medium sized jerrycan of siko were the alcoholic drinks also served on these occasions. All were reserved for any soldier or soldiers who might pass by or came to attend the wedding or spirit sacrifices, but no soldier had appeared since morning.

By the time Limlim's presence in the nearby village was established, one of the elders decided to increase the quantity of whatever was provided by the bride's relatives and to personally take them to Limlim – hence the many calabashes, gourds and jerrycans which accompanied the elder. The wedding guests were also few in number. The food and drinks prepared were more than enough for the day. In an expensive marriage like this the bride's relatives expect the bridegroom's relatives to come in large numbers. The amount of food taken to captain Limlim would also be an honor to him in front of his soldiers.

Captain Limlim was also expected to attend the bride price negotiations the following day. The elder also came to invite him to attend and to apologize for not finding him sooner. Limlim was an important person in the marriage of his friend.

Captain Limlim summoned his logistics officer to take charge of the newly acquired provisions. The force was to dine with the food and drinks provided. The force was to drink the two large jerrycans of siko, each containing four imperial gallons. The drink was more than enough for the whole unit. Most soldiers drink any type of alcohol, be it marisa, asilia or the hot siko made from sugar or dates. Siko is spirits and is flammable when exposed to fire.

Captain Limlim ordered his adjutant to make sure that all the guns were collected and stored in one place. A sentinel was to be posted to guard the store. No guns were to be issued until he gave the order. Limlim reasoned that the soldiers might get drunk and may cause harm to themselves. 'Let them use their fists if they intend to fight,' he thought.

Captain Limlim ordered a large fire to be lit. They were to feast around it that evening, perhaps until midnight. If possible they would try to recount some folktales or the dire actions undertaken by any of them such as the story which had been related to them in the morning.

The adjutant instructed one of the corporals to carry out the orders. The orders were adhered to and by early evening dinner was served. The calabashes containing asida bathed in cow's butter were the first to be consumed. There were four large calabashes filled up to the brim. Almost every soldier partook. Asida bathed in cow's butter is a coveted and rare delicacy to every Dinka. It is provided at every wedding. Several jerrycans full of cow's butter must be purchased by the bride's relatives if they do not have their own. Other dishes or calabashes were to be eaten after that to satisfy the soldiers.

A great fire was lit. All the soldiers sat around it and siko was apportioned to those present. A few soldiers declined and said they were not in the habit of taking beverages containing alcohol, not even marisa or asilia. But those were very few beginning with Captain Limlim and a young soldier named Giir. The rest of the force were consumers. The soldiers laughed and taunted the abstainers, saying, 'teetotallers oo yee, teetotallers oo yee.'

When all were duly warmed up, Captain Limlim suggested that someone relate a folktale, as our grandmothers used to do, or a harrowing situation that they had experienced. Many hands went up. Some even stood up to be better seen by the captain. One soldier named Wadaa stood and began to talk without being invited. Captain Limlim understood that when soldiers become drunk they become unruly, so he allowed Wadaa to relate what he had in mind.

WADAA:
A HUNTER AND RIIR[1]

‘O nce upon a time a very bad hunter lived near a forest. The forest lay between three villages. It was teeming with game. The hunter killed several animals each day. The big game sensed that they were being targeted and so they migrated to larger and denser forests. Only small animals and rodents were left. Even then the hunter went on killing them mercilessly. The small antelopes and gazelles were always on the lookout for the hunter. They escaped from his poisonous arrows when they saw him approaching. But the hunter hid himself in the bushes and once he had taken aim and

---

1   A *riir* is a very poisonous snake.

released an arrow, the animal fell down dead. He never missed his target.

'Finding no small game, for they quickly took flight when he approached, the hunter turned to rodents. He knew the footprints of everyone. He dug them out from their holes. Other small animals such as *digdig*, that is the rabbit, were not spared. The meat of the porcupine was a delicacy to him and he ardently searched for their footprints in order to dig them out and kill them. The small animals and rodents had a hard time. All lamented in unison, "What shall we do?"

One evening after the hunter had gone back home, all the animals and rodents called a meeting. "What shall we do with this hunter? The big game have left the forest because of this man. That was good for them but also a blessing for us because the lion, leopard and cheetah followed them. Only the foolish and gluttonous hyena has remained but he is not dangerous. The hyena does not venture out from his abode by day. It is only in the early evening that he leaves for one of the three villages. He comes back in the morning either contented with himself for having eaten enough or forlornly when he fails to find something edible."

What to do about the hunter was a difficult question to answer. How were they to come up with a practical solution to this menace? It was more than half an hour before anyone spoke.

Riir, the snake spoke first.

"I have a proposal. One of us must sacrifice himself for

the sake of the others. I call upon Iguana to die on behalf of the others."

Iguana protested, "Tell me, what do I need to do before I agree to become a sacrificial lamb?"

Riir said, "You must rush out from your hiding place when the hunter approaches. The place must be close to my hole. As soon as he sees you, the hunter will begin to aim at you. When you see him doing that, rush to my hole. Enter it without fear. With the rest of your body inside the hole, he will come running to get hold of your tail. When he begins to pull you out, I will jump out of the hole, wind myself around his neck, say a few words to him then bite him to death."

All the animals applauded the proposal. If it worked, that would be the end of all their woes.

Iguana agreed. He said, "The proposal is accepted but don't bite me when I rush to your den. You snakes do not like your tails being touched or remaining side by side with other animals."

The plan worked. Riir wound itself firmly around the hunter's neck. The hunter unwittingly went down, shivering all over his body with eyes protruding out of his head and mouth agape.

The fierce black eyes of Riir stared the hunter in the face. Riir's forked tongue flicked in and out of its mouth. The long poisonous fangs were poised to strike. Riir began to spit in the hunter's face. To avoid Riir's poisonous spittle, the hunter turned his head from side to side and closed his eyes. He could become blind if the saliva entered his eyes.

Riir began to question the hunter, "Why kill the animals at this alarming rate? If you value *your* life, then you should also value the life of the animals. Answer me before you breathe your last." But the hunter had no means of answering Riir's questions. He was about to suffocate because Riir continued to tighten his grip around the hunter's neck.

As the two were thus locked in that awful embrace, Awan the fox emerged from nowhere. He pretended to have suddenly stumbled upon them, struggling. He stood, startled, with his mouth open. The hunter's eyes were bulging out of his head and with an open mouth he could not talk or reply to Riir's questions.

Awan the fox said, "Can you give me a few seconds of your time Mr. Riir. I am a person who cannot leave two people struggling for dear life. I want to hear from each of you what is amiss. I have been watching the two of you since I emerged from the bush. I see the man cannot answer your questions. He is frightened and suffocating and you want him to answer you? You ask him why he has frequently killed many animals. Is it for food or for fun? You told him no animal is safe from his poisonous arrows, except Agok, the monkey."

Now the Dinka do not eat Agok's flesh or that of Awan the fox.

"I am also an enemy of man. They take me to be cunning and deceitful. I am even accused of stealing their chickens from the pens and maize during the rainy season. This man did not kill me because I hide earnestly from hunters, though he might have killed some of my kith and kin for their fur. Please give him a chance to answer some of your questions but be ready to strike in case he takes an arrow."

Riir answered, "Awan, what do you want me to do? Don't poke your nose into matters that don't concern you. Your sayings and deeds don't tally at all. Your tongue is forked. I don't want to listen to his lame excuses. What is he going to say? Killing five to ten animals a day has no excuse or reason. One animal is enough for his meals for several days. See all the big game has left this nice forest due to this man. The number of small animals and even rodents is daily dwindling also due to him."

Awan replied, "I am very much aware of all that you tell me but give him a chance to say something. He may tell us that he is not alone. Therefore, we should also be looking out for other enemies not yet eliminated. I agree with you but justice requires both sides to state their views. If you had not talked to him, I would not have solicited you to give him a chance to reply to your questions."

Riir replied, "How do I allow him to say nonsense? I don't have the stomach to listen to anything that comes out of his mouth."

"Just untie your grip around his neck, stretch yourself on the ground near him and let him say a word or two in reply to your questions. However, my man, if you make a move, that's your end. See Riir, I am taking away his damn bow and poisonous arrows."

The hunter usually carries a quiver full of arrows, a

bow with one arrow outside the quiver ready to shoot at an animal and a machete. After the bow and arrows were removed, Riir began to unwind itself, but remained ready to strike if the hunter made a move. Its black eyes were focused on the hunter.

But the sharp machete lay in front of the hunter. Riir did not know its use so he paid no attention to it. The arrows were the only danger to the animals. When they were removed, there was no longer any danger.

Awan said, "Hunter, before you answer Riir, *ye ngo, yee loi; ee weth ken*? (What do you do with this iron?)"

The hunter looked at the machete, snatched it up quicky and chopped off Riir's head.

Ngoth!!! *Ngoth*!!! "That's it," Awan said twice and vanished.

Everyone laughed and applauded Awan's deeds and hailed him for his craftiness.

CAPTAIN LIMLIM ALLOWS GIIR TO STATE HIS ORDEAL

S everal soldiers raised their hands to relate something or other. Captain Limlim requested someone who had had a narrow escape from imminent death or who had overcame a dire peril. Giir Yuol, a very quiet soldier and young by age, requested the captain to allow him to relate how his friend Nuul Kuel and he survived, some two years back, from sure death. They were coming back from Ethiopia. The two of them are still alive despite several battles they have been engaged in. His friend Nuul got wounded in one of the attacks. He still has the bullet between his ribs and his lungs.

Captain Limlim responded and allowed Giir to relate his tale. He asked the soldiers to remain calm and listen. He said, 'Returning from Ethiopia, either with many or a few soldiers often resulted in death for some. Be quiet and listen to Giir's tale. Sip your siko slowly. There is more of it in the cans. If you become drunk we will send you to bed and you won't get any more.'

Everyone became attentive and listened to what Giir had to say. Giir was not a talkative person. He was one of the teetotalers. He made sure that tea was available every day and he drank tea at an alarming rate even if there was no sugar. He used honey to sweeten his tea or drank it bitter.

Giir Yuol began, 'You are all aware how we went to Bilpham in Ethiopia and back to our country. We shall not dwell upon that. I want to relate what happened to me and what brought my friend Nuul back to rescue me, and how both of us escaped death miraculously.

'After our training ended, our brigade was ordered to leave for Bahr el Ghazal. There were over a thousand officers and men. My platoon or unit came last. All the units were ordered to walk in groups and to spend the night together in the same place. The distance allowed between one unit and another was less than two miles. We were to spend the night in the same fashion. Our platoon was tasked with taking care of all those left behind for one reason or another. The commander of the brigade was in the second group. Those in front were ordered to cover between five and ten miles per day if that were possible. Each soldier was heavily loaded with different arms and several boxes of ammunition plus personal belongings such as food, water canteens and sleeping things.

On the first day the company or platoon in front covered over twenty miles. They started in the early hours of the morning and did not stop till late after dusk. Every unit tried to keep pace with the one ahead of it in order to narrow the distance in between. Each platoon was forced to walk till the early evening hours or later. All the units were over stretched.

'Most units started to walk before daybreak on the second day in order to catch up with the unit in front. No unit rested, although the sun was very hot and fierce. Everyone became tired and exhausted. Thirst and hunger were also a menace. Most water canteens were drained before half the distance was covered.

'You know the wide barren savannah desert between Akobo and Pibor and between Ethiopia and the canal. It was the month of March. All the vegetation of the savannah desert, as people call it, had been consumed by fire. The inferno left no grass unburnt. You know that the area is treeless except in the few high places which were far from the route we took.

'The whole brigade walked midway between Akobo and Pibor. The distance between the two places is very great. The Nuer are to the right and the Murlei to the left when coming back from Ethiopia. The two tribes were anti-movement. They had established militias in order to intercept new recruits going to Ethiopia. They had killed several recruits and even trained army soldiers returning from Ethiopia, coming back to fight the Arabs.

'The two tribes were very hostile. They were heavily armed by the Sudan army. Several recruit convoys from Bahr el Ghazal were intercepted and eliminated beginning with Abdalla Chuol who killed over a thousand recruits from Bahr el Ghazal. Over a thousand others drowned in River Kiir when they tried to swim back to the western bank up to the time our brigade was returning.

'The Murlei or Nuer militia used to follow the soldiers returning to the theater of war by night. They killed those soldiers who from exhaustion, sickness, thirst or hunger, lagged behind. Sometimes the militia men kill the victim or victims right away and take their guns and whatever is useful for the journey. At other times the victim is left helpless. His gun, water, kit, clothes and whatever is edible is taken from him and he is left at the mercy of the sun, sickness, thirst and hunger. No person left in such a situation can survive. If the militia happened to be Nuer the victim was left alive. The Murlei do not spare him, but neither does the sun, sickness, thirst or hunger.

'The sun is merciless. It does not forgive. No shade of any kind is available anywhere from the Ethiopian border up to the canal. Only in a few villages enroute and they are usually deserted or avoided by travelers. Conflict between the tribes living in that part of Jonglei, between the Dinka,

Murlei and Nuer causes them to be abandoned. The three tribes raid each other from time to time to acquire cattle. Cattle rustling is the norm. It runs in their veins.

'In this savannah desert the eye sees far, and far away the sky merges with the earth. A few gazelles and antelopes graze here and there. What do those animals pick up from the bare ground? It is impossible to see. But still, they survive the drought. These small animals do not drink the whole dry season. Once the rain falls and stagnant water collects here and there those animals drink so much that they are not able to walk or run. The inhabitants of the villages catch the animals which graze nearby. The animals cannot escape. But their meat is said not to be tasty. It contains very little blood and water but something salivary covers the meat.

'People say that this vast Savannah turned desert was once a great thick forest, that the great floods of the early 1960's killed all the trees. The flood water remained in this empty area for several years, and only a few high places remained dry from year to year until the end of the flood. A few very old *alalop* "thou" trees survived but they no longer produce any fruit. They are crumbling and no new shoots spring up under them. When the flood receded and the area dried out, the inhabitants set the grass ablaze. It took several months before the fire was extinguished. The inferno turned the dead trees to ashes and left the place treeless.

'During the rainy season the opposite takes place. Grass grows very quickly, thick, dense and very tall. When we first went to Ethiopia in September or October, the grass was between two to four meters in height, and our convoy created a track about half a kilometer wide. The track we made was the only open space where one could see to the right or left. We made a wide open space where the grass was crushed to the ground. The grass in front of us was knocked down by the recruits who walked ahead of the convoy and they could not see what lay ahead of them.

'That is the area I fell sick in. We had walked for almost two days without rest when I was suddenly afflicted by a terrible bout of malaria. I collapsed and lay flat on my back in the hot noon sun and remained in that position for the rest of the day. No soldier was brave enough to stay with me from that time till midnight. All were mindful of the fate that awaited soldiers left behind. By the time I regained consciousness, Nuul arrived. He was among those who walked in front of our platoon. When the platoon halted for the night, Nuul came back for me.

'The soldiers had settled in groups to eat before going to sleep, but Nuul walked from one group to the other enquiring about my whereabouts. Those who left me lying there were not brave enough to tell Nuul what had happened to me. When the last group told him that I had been left behind sick, he became angry and sad. He left at once without returning to the people he led carrying only a Kalashnikov with a few rounds. The track that the soldiers walked in was wide and he walked from one end to the other calling out my name.

'Nuul put out of his mind what we were told – "the Nuer and Murlei militias come behind, following the forces in order to get the guns abandoned by the sick." It was mere luck that I had regained consciousness by the time he called my name. I replied to his call and he came to where I had fallen. When I recognized him, I became very sad and began to weep. "Why did you come back Nuul? It is not right that the two of us should perish in this place. Go back at once. I am not able to walk. Go back and tell our people how I died." But Nuul would not comply. He said, "Let us both die here! I cannot leave while there is breath still in your lungs." No matter how much I tried to persuade him, he would not budge. Instead, he lay flat on the bare ground where the grass was trampled underfoot. I asked him to spread one of my bed covers on the ground and lie on it. He refused to do that too and lay down as he had intended.

'Before the cock crew a group of militia men stumbled upon us. They were either Nuer or Murlei. The first two or three to come upon us immediately snatched our guns which were lying at our sides. After that they looted all that we had, ammunition, water kit, some food and my bag. Nuul was asleep. He awoke when one of the men stepped on his hand.

'Then they went back to their comrades. The rest of the men who stood some distance away surrounded them. They murmured in low voices. Three or four returned to us. They searched us all over and finding nothing went back again to their comrades who stood still in one place. They conferred again. One of them came back and threw a small thin stick near me and they all vanished as abruptly as when they arrived.

'We did not know whether they were Murlei or Nuer. None of them uttered a sound. We failed to see their faces or hear their speech. But the place they found us in was midway between the two tribal areas.

'I recovered a little before dawn. I asked Nuul to get up and suggested that we move ahead. "If the malaria does not come back again, we may reach the troops, within a day or two. We are ten to twelve hours behind." We carried nothing. We had no water or food to eat. We walked only four hours when I collapsed again. This time I did not recover for most of the day.

Nuul tried his best to make me comfortable and to protect me from the intense heat of the sun. He tried to cover some parts of my body especially my head with his own shirt but that was not able to reduce the terrible heat and besides that I had a high temperature from the fever. Nuul himself was suffering from the heat and thirst. By late evening I had again recovered a little. Nuul advocated walking back to Ethiopia. Ethiopia was nearer than Dinkaland or any area friendly to the movement. I refused and told him we should press on.

'After some hours of walking without resting, I collapsed a third time. I lay on my back till about four o'clock in the morning. Nuul sat by my side unable to do anything. We were very thirsty and hungry. When I recovered a little I asked him to let us press ahead before sunrise. We had covered about two miles when I collapsed and fell again. This time I lay as one dead.

'I don't know exactly what happened next. Nuul said he saw some small dome-like shacks some distance away from where I had fallen, and he went to investigate. When he returned he picked me up and carried me on his back with my legs dangling on the ground behind him. I became semi-conscious when my feet began to hurt. I opened my eyes and surveyed the scene before us. The village appeared deserted and devoid of human life, abandoned. Nuul continued to haul his load seeking a better shack for us to stay in, but before Nuul found what he was looking for, a woman emerged from one of the shacks. She was completely naked except for a few strings of beads tied around her waist, and middle-aged with flat skinny breasts.

'She could not communicate with Nuul orally as neither spoke the same language, but she managed to convey what she intended to say by using some deaf signs. Nuul did likewise. Having thus communicated she hurriedly returned to her shack and returned with a small gourd full of drinking water. I wanted to drink more than enough directly from the mouth of the gourd but she pulled it back and presented a small calabash cup, what we call a *biiny*. She measured out some water in the cup and handed it to me. Then she did the same for Nuul. After that she made a sign as if to say, "Let us move forward." Catching hold of one of my arms and signaling to Nuul to take the other, she guided us to where a hole had been dug in the earth to a depth of about two meters. She pointed to Nuul to go down first using a small ladder. Then the two supported me as I too descended into the cavern.

'The hole set deep in the earth was large enough to accommodate four or five persons. It was clean inside. The woman lowered the gourd of water after us and signaled to Nuul to not let me drink till she returned, while he, Nuul could drink as much water as he needed to quench his thirst. She had something else in store for me.

'Our benefactress returned after what seemed like an interminable interval, tapping on the ladder. I was almost dying of thirst by this time and had a high fever. She handed Nuul a small calabash cup, larger than the one she first measured out the water for us to drink. She instructed Nuul to let me drink the whole *biiny*. It was full of water which contained some herbal medicine, which had been crushed into powder. I took the whole lot at one draught. As soon as the drink hit my stomach, I began to feel something leaving every part of my body, and it all ended up in my stomach.

'The good woman knocked again at the ladder. She signaled to me to come out of the hole. She directed me to the far end of the shacks. Before reaching it, I began to feel bubbles and gases in my stomach which then converged in my rectum. Before reaching the area behind the shack,

I started to unbutton my trousers and squatted. Out of me poured all the water I had drunk and anything else that was inside me. It took some time before my intestines were emptied but I felt relieved and strong again. I felt sick no longer, now only thirsty and hungry.

'I rose to my feet and studied our surroundings. The place looked like the rest of the Savanah desert, monotonous and lifeless. Except for the few shacks jutting out the area was flat and as treeless and grassless as other parts of the Savanah.

'At the beginning of the rains the whole place turns green with grass growing everywhere. There are no trees. Thousands of wild animals return from the places they have migrated to. The land is populated again by life of every kind beginning with the few gazelles and antelopes which brave the hot sun, thirst and lack of pasture. The large game also come back, the elephants, buffalo, giraffes, rhinos and even their king, the lion.

'I returned to the hole and the woman came back carrying a large calabash full of hot steaming *wal wal*. She had placed upon the *wal wal* two small calabash cups or *biiny*. She signaled to us to eat while it was still warm. We consumed the lot. We then drank heartily, took our fill and lay down. Within seconds we were fast asleep. We remained so until late evening.

'To find such a powerful herbal medicine in such an arid and inhospitable place was a miracle. It was hard to imagine that a person lived there, especially a woman by herself, with all the kindness *Nhialic* (God) had granted her. No water could be found anywhere, near or far, but she provided us with the freshest, coldest and cleanest water in the best clean washed calabash cups.

'There was no sign of cultivation carried out here before or even during the last rainy season, but the woman offered us the best *wal wal* we had ever tasted. I cannot tell what she cooked it with but it was tasty up to the last morsel. The quality and quantity of *wal wal* should not have been made for strangers like us but she saw how hungry we were. The amount she provided should have been for her grown up and strong sons who had gone looking for something to bring back to the village to improve her life and theirs.

'The good woman did not see us as strangers but as her own children returning hungry from a long journey. She was an angel housed in this damnable semi-arid and inhospitable place to render help to strangers who arrived in peril of their lives. Nhialic should have blessed her with all the tongues spoken in South Sudan. The name, Mother South Sudan, should be bestowed upon her.

'The woman must have been a beauty in her prime. Her appearance suggested that. She was tall, slender, almost five and half feet with the kindest human face and heart almost impossible to get anywhere. Nhialic endowed her with qualities rarely found in most human beings. The good Nhialic should prolong her life to help all those left behind, the exhausted, the sick, thirsty, hungry and abandoned in Akobo's wilderness.

'The woman confined us in that hole probably for our own protection. When she tapped the ladder or made a sign for us to come out, she looked in all directions. She did the same when I went back after defecation. She must have been expecting the return of people who live there or normally frequent the place. Those persons might be hostile to us and that's why she kept us hidden during the hours of daylight.

'When she ordered us out the sun had already gone down but it was still relatively light. She stood near the entrance to the hole holding two gourds. One contained some boiled dura mixed with local beans and maize, while the other, which was larger, was filled with drinking water. She handed me the container of food and Nuul the other. She directed us using signs and her message was clear. "Don't walk at all during daylight hours no matter how hot the sun is. Sit in one place and remain there without moving. Walk at night, especially this night, without stopping or resting." Furthermore, we should use our food and water economically and make it last for three days and three nights. We shouldn't walk to the far right or far left but midway between the places the sun rises from and where it goes down. On the third day we might find people.

'She might have suspected us to be Dinka, even though none of us had tribal marks on the forehead. The Dinka of Bor, their neighbors, do not have special and regular marks like the Nuer. Some other Dinka people living among Nuer, Luac or Nyaraweng are marked in the same way as Nuer. The Nuer of Jonglei know very little about the Dinka west of Kiir River. They may not be aware that some of them have tribal marks which look like those of Nuer. Others, like Rek, Malual and other groups differ from theirs. She would have noticed that our lower teeth had been removed. This is also a Nuer custom. These were the thoughts that flashed through my mind.

'The woman bade us goodbye and signaled to us to leave and walk fast.

'I suspected the place to be a center for one of the tribes in the area during the rainy season. The ground was a little higher than its surrounds. However, it could not have been a cattle camp for we saw no cow dung or burnt ashes as we approached it. The cattle raiders probably gather here before heading off in the direction intended for cattle rustling. It is said that the Murlei when about to raid either the Dinka or Nuer, bury water in gourds along the route they plan to take when returning with the cattle. The raiders also know where drinking water is buried for use during the dry season. The Murlei are alleged to have very low fertility, especially their women. The cause has not been established by the medical people. To compensate for this, they buy children from their neighbors, the Dinka, the Nuer and the tribes of eastern Equatoria. It is also alleged that the Bor sell the children born by their daughters out of wedlock to Murlei. Those illegitimate children are disposed of by their maternal uncles. The number of cows paid for children varies. A boy fetches more cows than a girl or perhaps it is vice versa. I don't know which is which. They also increase their number by stealing children from their neighbors or by taking them captive during cattle rustling. Children bought or captured are cared for and brought up like their siblings. It is those bought or captured children, Nuer and Dinka who become ardent fearsome Murlei tribesmen or women when grown up. It is those children turned Murlei who come back to raid their kith and kin of the next generation.

'Cattle raids or rustling is a common cultural and social phenomena in this part of Jonglei and parts of Eastern Equatoria. The colonial government and various past Sudanese governments failed to stamp out the practice completely, but they did manage to reduce it somehow. Today, it is on the increase and it may take years to bring it back to an acceptable level.

'After ceasing sign language, the woman allowed us to leave and to quicken our pace. She moved her hands very rapidly with her beautiful fingers, moving them very fast to make us understand her meaning. She wanted us not to rest or stop for anything till morning. As soon as the sun rose we should not move. She also showed us how to apportion the water and boiled dura. She had fixed a small calabash with a string to the handle of one of the gourds. She handed us the two gourds and left.

'We walked into the unknown midway between east and west. We expected danger from every direction. We were spooked by the wilderness lying between hostile tribes. The nights to be spent on the way began with the one we left the Good Samaritan woman. We walked nonstop, not hearing or seeing anything around us, neither bird, nor insect nor animal. The whole place and the night were very quiet and dark. We feared stepping into danger, either from cattle raiders or cattle thieves.

'Come dawn we sat down to rest and slept till the sun was high in the sky. It was already hot. We followed the good woman's advice and did not move. We began to measure out the water before we ate a few measures of boiled dura. After eating this we took some more contrary to the good woman's directive. The place looked like the rest of the savannah without trees or grass. A few antelope and gazelle stood here and there in groups. I think it was their way of enduring the intense heat. They stood motionless for the whole day near one another with one of the males alone at the head of the herd.

'I reckon that the desert sun can be endured more easily than this. At least in the desert there are sand dunes where one can find some shade or an oasis where water is available. Here, there was none. But the inhabitants of this place know every nook and cranny of this vast vacant land. They can cut across it in a few days going on raid safaris or returning with booty.

'As for us, we had been warned. The Dinka, Murlei or Nuer, could be hiding elsewhere, some place we were not aware of. Once they spot us that could be our end…

maybe, except for the Dinka people. The Dinka would at first try to find out our ethnicity before inflicting harm upon us. As for the others they would not spare our lives, even if we pleaded with them. The Murlei and Nuer were anti-movement and the Dinka of Bor, their neighbors. A Dinka found in this place was either an SPLA soldier or one of those Dinka cattle thieves hiding or a path finder for the cattle rustlers. No mercy would be shown to any of these.

'We spent a very hot and uncomfortable day. No matter what we did there was no escape from the heat. Our shirts did not help even when we covered our heads. We sweated and sweated till there was no more moisture left in our bodies. We continued to measure out small amounts of water from time to time, to moisten our drying throats and tongues. But it didn't help. At sunset we set off after taking some small measures from one and the other gourd. Some amounts of boiled dura and water remained in each. I still carried the boiled dura and Nuul the water.

'This night we did not cover as much distance. We rested several times, more times than the good woman advised us. Each time we stopped, two measures of water and one measure of food was consumed. After four o'clock as we guessed the time, we sat down and rested. Instead of remaining seated we lay flat on the bare ground and in no time we fell asleep.

'Half an hour after closing my eyes I had a terrible nightmare. I dreamt I was swimming in a shallow river.

Then suddenly I began to sink. I went down twice, but the third time I rose above the surface of the water. I screamed and woke up, terribly shaken and shivering. I lay facing towards the west. When I opened my eyes, I was even more startled. In the far western horizon where the sky meets the earth, something impish was laughing at me showing its crooked fangs. It had a round face with eyes set deep under the brows.

'Suddenly a bright glittering specter emerged out of the darkness. It pushed up very clear and bright. I saw it looked like the sun. It began to run very fast to the south, appearing to me now and then. It slowed down a little as it approached south proper, then shot up again at the speed of a bullet, its light flickering from time to time till it was swallowed up in the east. Only its shining rays were visible above the horizon.

'Probably I was awake and mentally disturbed.

'It was a bad omen and fiendish. Stories connected to such scenes always have a bad ending leading to death, or if not, then some misfortune is bound to take place. A bad omen such as this is normally reported to the clan's elders. They would look for a man possessed by spirits, and that man's job would be to interpret and explain why such a spectacle should befall a person. That man is also the one who would tell the elders why the deities who may be angry has allowed other evil spirits to show the specter to their relative. That devilish abominable phenomenon appears once in a generation and only to those who are forsaken by the deities of the clan. Such is the belief of our people. The deities' intention is never healthy even if it does not result in death. But still a person who has seen such a specter expects misfortune.

'Our people have stories which say that at times early risers may encounter the sun, very early at dawn hurrying to its main base in the east before it begins to rise again. It is bad luck to see such a sight. It is evil to discern such an apparition. It is also related that the sun must have been delayed by evil spirits trying to punish the world for no good reason. But the creator rebukes and threatens them, allowing the sun to give its light to all his creatures. Once the sun is released it hurries at the speed of highway traffic from the far western horizon not visible to anyone's naked eye. Only unlucky persons are destined to be rebuked or taught a lesson by seeing it.

'Our people have these beliefs but I took them to be like any other imaginary and unfounded tales which concern good and evil. I told Nuul about it but in our situation we expected nothing more tragic to happen or for it to get any worse, except death. That we were going to die was a sure thing. If our enemies didn't kill us, thirst, hunger and fatigue would not spare us. Nuul would not comment and I didn't have the stomach to dwell on it. I was more worried about how we were going to survive the heat of the day.

'We chewed the last measure of boiled dura. The gourd was small and we had used up more than the Good

Samaritan woman had cautioned us to eat. Some water for the day and maybe part of the following night remained in the gourd.

'The day did not differ from the previous one. The vast monotonous flat land stretched out as far as the eye could see. Our eyes were unsteady. All was a blur. The sun had had no covering since we left Ethiopia and the shacks of the Good Samaritan woman.

'Evening arrived in the same manner as the previous ones. It was going to be our third night of walking. If we made it through the night, the following day would bring us near some friendly people or land.

'Starting from here, according to our benefactress' instructions, we were to turn west. So, we started to walk towards the west. Nuul said, "Let us not despair but to choose to live. We are only a few short miles from safety. By morning, if we walk without stopping to rest, daylight will find us in a friendly area."

'We again ventured into the unknown, mysterious darkness without sound of any living creature. A light wind blew from the north to the south. We felt relieved and increased our pace. We never looked upward to see whether the moon or stars were there. Without light we were unconcerned about that which might face us or attack us.

'We walked for several miles, then rested. After midnight it became difficult to lift a foot to make the next step. This went on for several hours. Each time we rested we took a drop of water to moisten our throats. You could not call it a drink. We reserved some water to cover part of the next day's needs.

'After the tenth stop and rest or perhaps more, Nuul got up. He told me to follow him. He had not covered thirty meters when I heard him calling, "Giir, Giir, Giir, kaac, kaac, duk buo, duk buo!!" repeatedly at the top of his voice. I heard something collapsing and a body flopping into a pit. He called to me from the bottom and I stopped a few paces from edge. Our gourd containing a little water had fallen with him and smashed into pieces. I stood shaking all over and probably Nuul was too. He again shouted to me not to come near. The pit or the place he fell into was about four meters deep. He could not see anything down there except the stars over his head. He could not catch hold of anything to climb up the sides of the pit to reach the top. We talked as much as we could. He could not hear me very well and I failed to get what he threw back up to me. We could do nothing now except settle down and wait for the sun to rise.

'I slept till after sunrise when I remembered what happened to us at night. I crawled on all fours to the pit as I still perceived it to be. Oh! It was the narrow part of the Jonglei canal, that long straight pit which stretched as far as the eye could see to the east and west of us. The canal had been excavated by small excavators making it large enough for the huge bucket wheel to move through in order to widen the canal to the required width. The excavated width of the narrow part was the size of the bucket wheel but the bucket wheel was far away.

'Nuul was sitting inside the canal four or five meters below, and I stood on the edge looking down at him. There was no way I could rescue him and Nuul had no means of climbing out. The hole was dug perpendicular to the surface of the land. It went straight down, and there was nothing for Nuul to catch hold of to climb out.

'At the bottom lay the skeletons of various mammals which had fallen into the channel and died there. Exhausted after running in either direction and finding no means of escape they crumpled up dead or succumbed slowly to thirst and hunger. There were also reptiles, some dead and some still alive. Especially hazardous were the snakes, pythons, various types of lizards and even scorpions. The frogs had buried themselves under the soil to avoid the sun's heat and save themselves from being swallowed by the hungry reptiles, the snakes and pythons.

'Nuul spied several reptiles coiled here and there, especially where flowing water had created a gully. None of them moved. Nuul was frightened. He was beset by many dangers. He had to tread very carefully when moving. The little water we had was gone. The gourd was smashed into pieces and we were separated. We had only a slim chance of surviving individually. We needed luck and we needed to encourage each other to overcome our difficulties. I edged closer to the lip of the canal in order to confer with Nuul. We agreed to walk westward during the hours of daylight. As soon as the sun went down Nuul was not to move as the canal was infested with dangerous creatures impossible to avoid in the dark. As soon as the sunshine was bright enough he should begin to walk. I would be moving above and would remain in contact with him below. I would tell him what was visible above. But there was nothing that could help us with the thirst, the hunger or the hot sun's heat.

'Below in the pit, according to Nuul it was as hot as it was above the pit. There were a few gullies eroded by rainwater but they were vertical and straight like the rest of the wall, and snakes had coiled themselves in most of them. It was not safe to try to climb out to the top through them. At the top where I was, the heat was as usual a blazing inferno. But across the channel to the north, abandoned machinery lay everywhere, huge bulldozers, dumper trucks, cars and lorries. They seem to have been abandoned when the work force was hurriedly evacuated. All were on the northern side of the canal. But to the south, where I was, no machine was left. The canal ran from the east to the west dividing the area in two, north and south.

'I told Nuul about this observation. I had no way of getting to the northern side of the canal as he had no way of getting out of it. In the north there would be shade to take cover in under those huge machines. Many of the machines had been vandalized or burnt by fire. Most of them I thought would not be useful again in the future. How I longed for the shade under them!

'Nuul walked westward inside the channel and I did the same at the top. We could not communicate for the sun's heat seemed to be more intense here. I was almost dying of thirst. I had to rest every hundred meters or less. I think Nuul was struggling down in the pit in the same manner.

'After covering about three miles, an abandoned camp on the northern side of the canal became visible to my blurry eyes. I went near the edge of the canal and informed Nuul. The camp might save us but how were we going to reach it? Neither of us could think of a way to get there or how we could ever be together again. I felt dizzy.

'My movements did not improve. I remained sitting longer and longer in the same place. I covered a few yards then lay stretched out on my back till evening. I think I managed about two miles from two o'clock to sunset. At sunset I lay down drowsy tossing to and fro. Thirst and hunger were severe. I even failed to contact Nuul as we had agreed in the morning. I tossed and turned dosing in one place most of the night. In the early hours of the morning, I got up and walked unsteadily westward. I had no idea why I was moving. My mind was fuzzy and death was imminent. I did not worry about when it was going to get me and maybe also Nuul. A light cool wind blew from the south to the north. It was cool and soothed me. It encouraged me to walk.

'After walking about a kilometer, I suddenly fell into a low place below the flat surface of the ground. I rolled and rolled. I was unable to stop myself. I allowed myself to roll till I could go no further. I had closed my eyes expecting to breathe my last. When I stopped rolling I opened my eyes. I saw steps leading upwards to the northern side of the canal. I also looked up to where I had rolled from and saw steps coming downwards to within a few feet of where I sat. There was a flight of steps to the south and another opposite to them a little farther away from where I sat to the north. Each went up to the surface.

'I remained seated in that position till I could see fairly well in all directions. I went up northwards crawling on all four till I reached the top. I returned in the same way and went up again southward on all four. I came back to the center of the channel, sat down and waited for sunrise.

'When I could see in all directions, I went up the steps southward again to the surface. Instead of going to Nuul by walking down the canal, I started along the top as before calling his name. I met him somewhere coming westward. I told him the good news. I said he should hurry to the exit point, while I would do the same at the top.

'But the discovery of the exit point did not improve our movements. It took more than two hours for the two of us to arrive at the exit. Nuul crawled out of the canal on all fours. I went down the canal on my bottom and arms. Ascending the north side, I used all four till I arrived at the top.

'I found Nuul sweating and palpitating. He had nearly fainted. The sun was getting hot. I sat near him till he recovered. He spoke to me feebly. I said to him, "I can see some houses and abandoned machinery ahead of us. If we can reach them we will find shade and perhaps a passerby can rescue us even if nobody lives in them."

'But he and I could not move. The sun was getting hotter and hotter. To us hell was no hotter. Our throats were totally dry with not the slightest saliva to moisten them. After half an hour, a slight cool wind blew. Its coolness encouraged us to get up, shaking and walking unsteadily towards the houses. After covering half a kilometer, we each went down and crawled forward on all fours till our trousers were torn and the skin on our knees was ripped open. We could not feel the pain or see the bleeding wounds. The sun's heat burned the wounds and they became numb. The wounds were bleeding with several blisters here and there around the kneecaps. After a mile or two, neither of us could move. I lay stretched on my stomach facing downward. I think Nuul might have been in the same position. Each of us lost consciousness.

'In the morning I felt something painful in my left arm. I did not open my eyes. It was like a dream but the pain persisted so I opened my eyes. To my surprise I found myself in a Red Cross medical facility. The first thing I said was, "Nuul ako!, Nuul ako!" I think I repeated it maybe ten times. A nurse, who was seated near us since we were brought in, signaled to me to be quiet. She pointed to Nuul lying opposite with a bottle of saline hanging above his head. The same thing was above my head. They both hung from the same stand.

'We had been rescued and were being taken care of by the International Red Cross. I went back to sleep with a smile on my face. Ten days or more passed before we were able to leave our hospital beds.

Lino Angok Kuec
Kuajok
September, 2013

THE KIKUYU
GENTLEMAN I MET

CHAPTER ONE

I recall a saying by a Kikuyu gentleman I met in Nairobi in 1999 when I paid a visit to that city for the second time in my life. I had lost a lot of weight and size. The usual size of my trousers became too large for me.

I entered the shop of a Kikuyu man and the trousers he showed me looked large although its number was smaller than the size I used to wear.

The man took me to his room behind the shop to undress and to try on the new trousers which I wanted to buy. After putting back on my old worn-out trousers, I asked the man about his tribe. I had been told that the Kikuyu are the meanest, the stingiest and the most selfish people in Kenya. No Kikuyu would invite a person to his home, let alone take a person to his room.

I was very much skeptical about the alleged claim but as a foreigner I wanted to prove it. So, I had to ask the gentlemen. The gentleman told me, "I am a Kikuyu, the largest tribe in Kenya. And if you go to the graveyard, you will find us the majority there." I laughed hard and long. I told him, "I am a Dinka, the largest tribe in the Sudan and if you count the number of war combatants, those killed in the present war and those alive and still carrying arms, the Dinka are the majority."

The Kikuyu gentleman invited me to sit down on the bed. I sat on it. He wanted me to talk to him about the war raging in South Sudan – the causes and the reasons for such a long war. The Kenyans are even feeling its effects.

When I finished what I thought the gentleman wanted to know, the Kikuyu gentleman went on to say that they, the Kikuyu, fought the Liberation War for Kenya's independence. "Ninety per cent of all those who carried arms against the colonizers and the settlers and those who died were our young people. The other ten per cent were the others. I trust you have heard about the Mau Mau movement in Kenya."

I told him that I had heard and read about it. I had even read 'The Trial of Jomo Kenyatta' and Kenyatta's book, 'Facing Mount Kenya.' Some of our people fled to Kenya in the early 1960's. Kenyatta wasn't friendly or sympathetic to our cause. He rounded up all those who fled and were seeking refuge and dispatched them back to Khartoum.

At the time of the Mau Mau movement and the war for Kenya's independence, I was a young teenage boy in intermediate school. African political movements such as the African National Congress (ANC) of South Africa, Kwame Nkrumah of the Gold Coast (then People Convention Party or PCP) and so on were the subject of daily discussions by the boys after preparation and when dinner was over. We were disgusted with the Sudanese political parties, the National Unionist Party (NUP), the UMMA, the People Democratic Party (PDP) and the Southern Liberal Party.

The Liberal Party was the sole southern party for southerners. I was a supporter of it. No northern Sudanese joined it while several southerners were in the northern parties. The Liberal Party had no money to support its members. The northern parties had lots of money to bribe the poor southerners who changed benches from time to time. The rich Arab countries poured a lot of money into northern parties, especially Egypt, and they bought the votes of our members.

The Sudan achieved independence in 1956 but we southerners were not happy. A new colonial era began. Southern teachers put in a word or two against our new masters. A new slavery was in the air. It was also the time we learned about the shrinking British Empire where the sun never used to set. Kenya, Tanganyika and Uganda achieved independence while I was still in intermediate school or in the teachers' institute. I can remember, if I am not mistaken, that a certain captain John Okello rattled the three East African countries mentioned.

Okello and Captain Abdu Karumah staged a coup d'état against the Sultan of Zanzibar. The coup nearly engulfed the three east African countries. Kenya and the other two requested Britain, the previous colonial power to come, as I recall, to their aid. I think Britain ferried in troops in order to stop Okello's movement spreading further. Tanganyika and Zanzibar later united and the country became known as Tanzania, as it is at the present day. Okello's movement was perceived to be Communist, inspired by the West.

The Kikyuyu gentleman told me further that after the war they were nowhere to be seen when the reins of power were handed over to the Kenyans. "Others who got educated while we fought the war occupied the lucrative civil service positions vacated by the English including even the police and the army. All those units needed educated personnel. The Kikuyu were not educated.

"For us, the Kikuyu, Kenyatta was at the helm but under him were others. We the Kikuyu brought about the freedom of Kenya but we were not able to enjoy the fruits accruing from it.

"It was due to the hard work and struggle of our young men and women that victory was achieved and it was assumed that the Kikuyu would constitute the majority in the government of Kenyatta.

"That might happen to your people. As you remarked before, your young men are now in the battle fields facing the enemy while others are attending classes of learning. By the time freedom is achieved, your young people will find no positions to occupy, let alone juicy ones.

"They will be branded as uneducated, incompetent, inexperienced and not capable of running an institution. If a few get positions they might be mirror ones – the flesh and oily parts will go to others who are now studying in foreign universities or are boozing in foreign cities."

I failed to take the gentleman's remarks seriously but he had a message for me, a message now more serious than the way the man put it. I am now face to face with what the gentleman told me in a friendly way.

The Kikuyu gentleman then wanted to find out how much I knew. The questions he put to me were framed in such a way that seemed to doubt my credibility and the extent of my knowledge. I think he was learned but younger than me. I talked to him at length about history and geography, not only that of Africa but of the world at large as well as my main subject which was English. He had no interest in English or its literature.

So, I talked to him about the East African countries of Kenya, Uganda and Tanzania. I told him how Kenyatta, Nyerere and Obote succeeded in achieving independence for their three countries. Kenyatta and Nyerere had socialist ideas and theories which the people of Kenya and Tanzania will have to evaluate as to their success or failure. To us in other countires they sounded very nice and attractive; Harambe in Kenya and Ujaama in Tanzania. However, Obote was hostile to the South Sudan movement, the Anya-nya. The late Fr. Santurnino Lahure met his death at the hands of Obote's security personnel in 1967.

I also talked to him about the three big men of central Africa, who dismantled the federation of Rhodesia and Nyasaland, Kaunda, Nkomo and Banda. Kaunda went away with Northern Rhodesia and renamed it Zambia. Banda likewise sliced out Nyasaland and renamed it Malawi.

Most of the whites in the two countries which became independent seemed to have moved to what was then known as Southern Rhodesia. Nkomo and Abel Mazerewa struggled within the country but failed to achieve freedom. It was Robert Mugabe whom many of us had never heard of who freed the country from white rule.

In the rest of Africa, Nkrumah was the first African leader to gain independence for his country, the Gold Coast. The country became known as Ghana. Nkrumah was a Pan-Africanist. He was far ahead of his time. What he preached at that time was not received in the mid-fifties but could have meaning for today. When Ghana gained independence in 1957, the rest of Africa, then known as the Dark Continent, was under white rule.

South African blacks were suffering under minority white rule. The ANC is probably the oldest African Party formed several years before we were able to read and write. South Africa became well-known through a book written by a white man called 'Cry the Beloved Country.' The book was so popular then that every young person read it. Another book written by the ANC leader, Chief Albert Luthuli, 'Let My People Go' was also popular but not to the tune of 'Cry the Beloved Country.' South Africa's black woes came to a climax when the apartheid police shot down several miners at Sharpeville. The World was shocked and alarmed. Several voices condemned white minority rule including their western allies.

I also told him about the Congo crisis of the 1960's. The first UN peace keeping force in Africa was in Congo. The Secretary General of the UN, Dag Hammarskjold, lost his life in a plane crash in Zambia while trying to pacify Congo. Patrice Lumumba, the first prime minister of independent Congo also lost his life due to rivalry between the world powers. He was suspected of being a communist sympathizer by the western powers.

I also told him how all the French colonies were granted independence but within the French sphere of influence. Only one country, Guinea of Ahmed Sukatore, opted out of France's sphere of influence. France had to disown the country totally but Nkrumah of Ghana came to his aid.

I also mentioned a few things about the first and second World Wars and the dropping of the first atomic bombs over Japan at Hiroshima and Nagasaki. The two World Wars were probably started by Germany. The Germans are a warlike people. It was they, the Germanic tribes, which destroyed the Roman Empire.

Japan was also a warlike country. She had a lot of colonial tendencies. Japan occupied China and Korea and other countries in the Far East. Japan's imperial attitude allied her to Germany in the second war. When Germany surrendered, Japan and the USA and her allies were still at each other's throats in the Far East and in the Pacific. The atomic bombs brought Japan to its knees.

The Kikuyu and I sat on opposite beds in his room. I think he began to take me seriously. I went on to tell him that during my school days, books on every subject were available and abundant. All that the teachers did was to tell every student to read two or three books per week and give the teacher a written summary for correction.

In geography we covered the whole world – political, economic and physical. We knew all the oceans and seas, the major shipping lanes, major industrial areas, major rivers, cities, railways, major wheat growing areas such as the Pampas in South America, the Prairies in North America, the Steppes in Russia and so on, major dense forests, the great mountains of the Himalayas, Everest and the great deserts of the world, the Sahara, Kalahari, and Gobi.

Before I returned to talk about the Sudan, I told him that I visited Kenya in 1978 when Kenyatta was alive. Nairobi was very much cleaner that it is today in 1999. During my first visit to Kenya, I bought a small book which I valued very much. The book was written by a Kenyan woman and titled, 'What does a Man want from a Woman.' It was the first book I bought when I arrived in Nairobi three or four days ago. The other books I need I have failed to find in the bookshops I have visited. They are Voltaire's 'Candide,' 'The Longest Day' or the day the allies landed in Normandy in June 1944 and the 'Six Day War,' about the Arab-Israel war of 1967.

Concerning my home, I talked to him at length about our differences with the Arabs. This has existed since time immemorial. The Arabs sold our people into slavery by the thousands. Now they are doing the same thing, besides killing our people in the hundreds of thousands and taking away our cattle wealth.

I have witnessed violence, ethnic cleansing, genocide and atrocities committed by the Arabs' Army and the Jalaba since the Torit Mutiny, from 1955 up to this day. But our history with the Arabs and Muslims from the past is worse – the slave trade, the Turkia and the Mahdia.

The Arabs want us to be subservient second-class citizens without rights in an Islamic state. In an Islamic country a non-Muslim has no rights over a Muslim even in a court of Law.

A Christian cannot be a ruler. A Christian cannot be a President or Prime Minister in an Islamic country. The Constitution doesn't allow it. In certain circumstances, a Christian or in most cases in our context where many of our people have their own traditional religion and beliefs, might be allowed, but they will be required to pay a certain amount of money to the State in order to be protected by the Islamic

State. Since independence in 1956 the South has never co-existed peacefully with the North even during the ten years of the Addis Ababa Agreement. The South was usually awarded minor ministries that no northern parties wanted.

Our problem with the Arabs is twofold, racial and religious. Our African brothers in the north who are Muslims were against us in the past. It was they who did most of the fighting and killing. It is only recently or in this present war when they felt racial discrimination and marginalization. They were fed with Islamic propaganda. They would be given the best places in heaven in the next life while the Arabs advanced themselves and their areas in this life.

The Arabs do not accept us as sharers of the country. To them the country is theirs and theirs alone. Their allegiance is to the Arab and Islamic World without regard for us Southerners who are not Arabs. We are even taken for granted to be members of the Arab League and the Islamic Countries Organization. The Sudanese Arabs know the Arab and Islamic world and its history better than that of the Sudan they live in.

As Muslims they do not tolerate any other religion and want all the South Sudanese to embrace Islam. Most of our people who are now inside the country and want to get political positions in the government must become Muslims. Many of them have embraced Islam to secure political posts.

In the past a Christian who converted to Islam had to take an Islamic name. Today they become Muslims while retaining their former Christian or native names. It is rumored that those who have embraced Islam during these years are branded with the crescent, the symbol of Islam, on their buttocks or thighs.

These renegade South Sudanese hide from people on Fridays when going to Friday prayers and think that what they do is not known.

We southerners are black Africans and mostly Christians. Even our native people at home admire Christianity. They detest Islam which they equate with slavery, the Turkia and the Mahdia, under which many of our people were sold into slavery and harshly treated.

We would have continued had the small boy he left to mind the shop not come to call him. I didn't see the man again till I left Nairobi three months later.

My talk with the Kikuyu gentleman wiped away the prejudice other people made me believe about the Kikuyu. It was a generalization. Not all Kikuyu are mean, selfish and bad. Those who talked to me might have encountered one or two bad ones then went on to generalize about all of them from that encounter.

I sat in the room of the Kikuyu gentleman. We had chatted for almost an hour. The encounter nullified what others had told me about the Kikuyu. What the gentleman did not do was to offer me a cup of water, or tea or soda which we usually do in the Sudan. It was not only the Kikuyu gentleman who did not do that but all Kenyan people do not offer such things to visitors, especially in public offices.

CHAPTER TWO

The talk with the Kikuyu gentleman took place several years before the CPA (Comprehensive Peace Agreement) was signed. I said earlier in this piece that I came face to face with what the Kikuyu gentleman told me.

I began to encounter something of what the Kikuyu gentleman told me as soon as the peace agreement was signed. I came to analyze what the Kikuyu gentleman meant by 'others', 'they', 'us' and 'we'...

I took 'others' and 'they' as the non-Kikuyu and 'we' and 'us' as the Kikuyu. In my context, 'us' and 'we' stand for the Dinka people and 'others' and 'they' as the other tribes. Our number 'us' although largely uneducated, unskilled and inexperienced still matches the 'others' and 'they' who had acquired better education and qualifications during the long years of the struggle. What the gentleman did not tell me was that the 'us' and 'we' have a lot of differences among themselves just as 'others' and 'they' differ among themselves and with 'us' and 'we'.

South Sudan is a semi-federated country where the ten states have their own governments with local civil administrations to run. Some local positions which should have been awarded through fair competition with education and experience at the foremost were shared out through misunderstanding after the Comprehensive Peace Agreement (CPA) was signed. Instead of political positions only, *all the positions* in the civil service in the state governments were put in a pool and shared out equally. Less educated persons with little or no experience compared with 'us' and 'we' filled positions allocated to 'us' and 'we'. Letters of educational qualifications and experience were dumped into the dustbins.

Newly graduated young people were pole vaulted into leadership positions in the civil service in order to let relatives and section men equalize with the learned and experienced persons of other areas. "The position is ours, we must fill our positions whether people from other areas like it or not." Traders who could not read or write were ordered out of their shops and appointed to leadership positions which were awarded to 'we' and 'us'.

On the other hand, the same 'us' and 'we' relatives, sons or those from our sections who had little education and who went abroad raw, were ordered to come back and placed in leadership and technical positions. Those relatives who went to foreign countries in order to save their skins and escape the suffering which the people left behind underwent and who had dual nationality were called back and placed in positions by their relatives and section men in power. And it was said, "They are not able to perform anything in the positions."

Many returnees from the diaspora came back as raw as when they went but the euphoria of seeing them return from Europe or America made our people believe that they came back highly learned and better educated than the graduates from home universities who were already known to the people.

Aspects of the 'us' and 'we' which the Kikuyu gentleman did not expand upon may not have been part of the Kenyan experience, appearing as a new phenomenon in our country and especially in the states.

The 'us' and 'we' who were diehard National Congress Party supporters of Omar al-Bashir because "he/she is a relative from our section," is awarded a prestigious position his former master never thought of giving to him or her. A person who supported the enemy one hundred percent and even participated in the elimination of freedom combatants is preferred to a freedom fighter, because "he/she comes from our area," an area he/she would have burned to ashes and killed his own people entrapped there, had he had the chance to do so and which some of them did.

Some among 'us' and 'we' embraced Islam and danced to the tune of al-Bashir's drums, to eliminate and annihilate the infidels who were against Islam and the country. It was they, alone, who were going to be left to start the propagation of a new Dinka species and other southern tribes. They would be subservient to the Arab race and Islam, a people if asked before the CPA, would have sided with the enemy. Now it is they who are enjoying the fruits of freedom which they would have plucked from the freedom fighters' hands and handed over to their Arab masters.

Moreover, 'us' and 'we' are those who remained in the government held towns and cities. Many of them were supporters and members of al-Bashir's National Congress Party (NCP). As soon as the CPA was signed, al-Bashir's outgoing governors awarded every one of them an accelerated promotion in order to bar those who joined the movement and who were senior to them before their defection.

The movement's caretaker governors and the governors appointed after them who took over the reins of power from al-Bashir's men forgot that there was a Civil Authority of New Sudan (CANS) in the liberated areas with all the established rank and file of government machinery but they were not paid any salaries or wages.

Because the officials found in the Sudan Government-held towns and cities had money, they knew how to manipulate the leaders in power. The caretaker governors had their pockets filled and so they danced to the tune of al-Bashir's men and officials.

The same governors appointed after them, likewise, got lost in what was handed to them by al-Bashir's men. They totally forgot the officials and workers who were with them in the bush. The poor newly appointed commissioners were left with both their counties' staff and those of the state. The commissioners did not know what to do with the large staff left in the countryside. The state governors and ministers became very comfortable with al-Bashir's staff.

Instead of the movement's personnel absorbing the NCP staff, as was stated previously by the late Dr. John, the opposite became the norm. The status quo was retained and the officials and workers who played a role in the liberation movement were side-lined. They remained at the mercy of those who were al-Bashir's right-hand men. A tragedy. Many of them have not recovered up to the present day.

CHAPTER THREE

T he Kikuyu gentleman's talk became clear and began to make sense to me. The businessmen and women who supported the movement with their own wealth during hard and difficult days were side-lined, and wealth accrued to those persons who did not lose a cent or contribute anything to the war effort.

Our kith and kin who contributed nothing (not even to help a soldier carry a box of ammunition or offer a cup of water to a tired, sick and dying soldier or offer a he-goat to starving soldiers on their way to the front), were placed around the juicy, well-dressed tray, full of cakes to help themselves to… "The pie goes first to our relatives."

I know a certain Musa Anei Ajiec who contributed a great deal during those difficult and hard years. He was thrown into jail for money he had borrowed to support the peace talks in Tonj. Anei provided fuel and spare parts for the vehicles of the movement when he was in Mayen Rual. It is shameful that a man who offered his wealth for the freedom of this country should have been allowed to go to prison. The money he spent to feed the chiefs and all those who attended the conference was not paid back to him. I shed tears for Anei's suffering and mistreatment. The movement's supporters and activists are treated like trash.

'Us and we' who contributed nothing to the movement get very fat cheques every month, payment for imaginary roads and bridges constructed. The cheques might be split into two.

The businessmen who fed others, provided fuel, lubricants and spare parts for the tanks and cars of the movement, do not approach the leaders in power, be they in the central government or the states. A ring of good-for-nothing jesters and cronies surround the leaders. They do not allow anybody to pass through the thick net wound around the leaders. All that the leaders hear is, "Everything is in order and fine. Everybody is happy with you and supports you, and wishes you to remain where you are."

Even in the rank and file of the movement's fighters, supporters, jesters, cronies and protectors have developed around the leaders and the party. To them, other members are not committed or are unreliable because they joined the party late and for their own benefit. The daily gossip and lying encourages the leaders to practice cronyism where they could have been fair if they were not reminded from time to time to help so and so, a relative or a friend or a brother of so-and-so supporter.

The so-called guards who turned out to be jesters, cronies and protectors of the leaders have woven a tight web around the leaders, so much so that an honest South Sudanese with a clear mind, honest and with good intentions for the welfare of the country at heart, is prevented from seeing or meeting a leader. Even the religious leaders have hurdles placed before them to prevent them from meeting the leaders. Their mission is to voice the concerns of the people and to remind the leaders about Christ's peace and justice, that the leaders offer equal and just treatment to all South Sudanese citizens without distinction or favor.

Acts of violence and murder are committed by persons said to be close to the leaders including their own kith and kin. The culprits are not apprehended because they escape to the dens of the leaders. Many kidnappings have been committed by persons alleged to be close to people in high places and nothing is done to them. Lord Jesus Christ, save the country called South Sudan. Lord pour your spirit upon the leaders to govern your people justly. A writer once wrote, "The South Sudanese are their own worst enemy."

A South Sudanese who questions the rampant corruption in the country is the one the illicit wealth seekers do not want to see near any leader or to be alive. Those who highlight corruption, nepotism, tribalism, sectionalism and any other "ISMS" known to all of 'us', 'we' 'others' and 'they' are kept at bay and are termed non-SPLM supporters. Many of them are blacklisted and maybe subjected to imprisonment or removal from party membership.

Corruption is not new in the world. It is when it becomes uncontrollable, when people with good intentions for the welfare of the country become alarmed and very much concerned, that something needs to be done.

I once talked to a friend of mine in 2003 in Maridi. "How are we going to combat the rampant corruption which has engulfed the movement?"

My friend and roommate was a captain in the military. He was the headmaster of a prestigious southern secondary school at that time. He was a university graduate with vast knowledge of the country and the movement. He told me that corruption would cease to be as soon as peace was achieved. I laughed a long time and said to him, "An old bent tree cannot be easily straightened." It is what is very much apparent today. You see and meet people with badges who are wolves in sheep's clothing and the worst. To them, stealing public money is the only known form of corruption. However, placing unqualified sons, relatives and section men and women in positions they are not qualified for.. to them this is not corruption. Cronyism is as rampant as other corrupt practices. Paying salaries to ghost employees.. to them again this is not corruption.

Granting contracts to businesspeople without capital or technical know-how.. to them this also is not corruption. Most roads, bridges and other construction projects have come to a standstill. Projects are not started and public money is poured into bottomless pits, work stops and still more money continues to pour into them and no one is questioned.

CHAPTER FOUR

'Us' and 'we.' In one of the states a new governor was appointed. The new man brought with him a bunch of relatives, friends, section men and women and county men and women. The governor brought them in order to find places of work for them. The cronies were mostly semi-literate. Finding jobs for them became rather difficult. Cronyism may sometimes require the rudiments of reading and writing. However, finding no way out, the said governor resorted to sectionalism. The people from his section and county were not represented in any ministry or department. So, he decided to pool all the positions in the state government together. The officials and workers found in a ministry or department were asked to state their county and area of origin.

In the Secretariat General department of the state, three officials from one county were found. The governor asked the three to make room for two other persons from other counties. The governor thought he had devised a very clever way out. The three officials from the one county were asked to draw lots. The official the lot favored, would be the one who would continue to work in the secretariat. In the Bible the Apostles cast lots to fill the position vacated by Judas the betrayer of Jesus, a story which the governor might not have come across.

Maybe a die was used or cards. Probably prayers were conducted to let the Lord decide on the one the governor wanted. However, the three men were learned and experienced officials. They declined to draw lots. They told the governor to let the younger person from among them remain. So, two of them quitted their positions in the secretariat. They did not even ask for the three months grace period. The governor, then, had to place the bunch of persons who came with him, into the positions vacated by the two officials. These relatives had no knowledge about what they were going to do.

The same governor was once told about scholarships granted to students in the ten states. The state ministry of education asked students to apply whose certificates fulfilled the conditions needed by the university which was offering the scholarships. The scholarships were for a South African University. The said governor, instead of enquiring from the state ministry of education how scholarships awarded are filled, immediately nominated his own son and a message was sent to Juba to that effect. The governor's son's certificate could not even find him a room in one of the home universities. The boy did not pass his secondary school leaving certificate. The governor thought that the child of a governor must be eligible to enter any university his father desired. If he had become a governor with very little education, his son who went to secondary school had every reason to be awarded the scholarship meant for the state.

The state lost the scholarship.

The same governor thought his powers knew no bounds. He spent the money meant for the salaries and wages of the state officials and workers, at will without any authority asking or questioning him. The same man once boasted *ok abe rot aa wel biok kua yic, ke ho muk baany,..* that they would remain in power, "till they are not able to turn round in their old age beds." To him they would not relinquish power to anybody. One does not know who he meant when he used the word *ok* meaning 'we.'

All these observations I have jotted down here are about 'us' and 'we'. I do not know how 'others' and 'they' fare. I think my knowledge, experience and observation with 'us and 'we' may also be apparent in their circles. I take it to be the same, for we are all southerners and public money comes from the same treasury with the same persons signing approvals and payments to the same unseen, unchecked, uninspected and uncompleted projects' bills.

The disease called corruption is serious, endemic and it appears to be incurable and on the increase. "We, us, others and they" are all involved and we all point fingers at each other. To 'others and they', it is 'us and we' who are the most corrupt and worse than Arabs. 'Us and we' are accused of flowing to their areas and grabbing their land.

As for 'us and we', it is the 'others and they' who are the worst, the most corrupt and inconsiderate. The others and 'they' left 'us and we' to fight the war of independence almost alone. 'Others and 'they' even turned against 'us and we.'

Now, they do not want 'us' and 'we' to partake of our rightful share, something equivalent to our suffering and loss which occurred to 'us and 'we' in the form of lives and property.

The land, the 'others' and 'they' say is grabbed, was liberated by 'us' and 'we'. A few from among 'others' and 'they, fought hard side by side with 'us and we.' We don't deny their contribution but to equate 'us and we' with those who did not throw a stone at an Arab is not reasonable. When the Arabs took the land, nobody talked. Why now?

In the war 'us and we' died like flies and nobody complained. Peace was brought about by 'us and we' because 'us and we' never surrendered to the Arabs. Some among 'us and we' turned against 'us and we' and allied themselves with the Arabs. However, 'we and us' fought them together with the enemy till they came back to the rank and file of the movement.

The majority of 'us and we' never gave in to the enemy. How many renegades went over to the Arabs and came back? If all 'us and we' behaved in the same manner, this country would still be under the yoke of the Arabs and Islamist imperialists.

Many 'others' and 'they' sided with the Arabs and received freedom on a platter. They even stabbed 'us' and 'we' in the back. Or fought side by side with the Arabs. However, 'they' and 'others' still have grudges against 'us and we' despite the losses we have endured in lives and property.

However, that is not a warrant for 'us' and 'we' to take from 'others' and 'they' whatever they rightfully deserve. Fairness, justice and respect for the rules and laws laid down to govern the country should bring about political and social harmony and peace to all the people of South Sudan. And that is what 'others' and 'they' and 'we' and 'us' should all crave for. Let 'us', 'we', 'they' and 'others' all forget the grudges which have no firm foundation.

CHAPTER FIVE

The central government in Juba, I think is dominated by 'others' and 'they.' As for 'us' and 'we,' although we appear to be many, it is our sheer numbers, one from here and one from there. When put together the number swells and 'we' and 'us' become the majority. Take one official from each of the seven states we are found in, how many would 'we' and 'us' be to the 'others' and 'they?'

In an article which I wrote some years back, or a year after independence, I proposed a federal system like that of Nigeria. I suggested twenty states instead of the present ten, a central government under an executive president to rule the country for two terms of five years each, and after that he/she should not contest again.

I think the article was published but received no comments from the readers and other concerned persons who have the welfare of this country at heart. But today, some people are talking about it. 'Others' and 'they' and 'we' and 'us' would compete only for positions in the central government, preferably through examinations and not by favoritism or cronyism as is done today.

I wanted to solve a problem. The question of numbers, who are more here or there, will be understood. 'Us' and 'we' will still rank first in our own states and even in the central government. Our number, even with the examination would still put us ahead of 'others' and 'they.' One person from each of the seven states will add a lot. Our presence in the central government would still remain high.

There are many ways to the solve the problem of numbers in the central government. One of them should be through examination and another by quotas to be granted equally to each state no matter how small its population or its wealth. Let the job seekers in each state complete through the exams to fill their quota. In this way, finger pointing, resenting and backbiting may be reduced, if not eliminated entirely. These measures will not satisfy all the people. Today, the ministries in the central government are shared on an equal basis but still there is dissatisfaction.

As for the head of the state, that is South Sudan, if possible the constitution of the country should be worked out in such a way that the three old Southern provinces of Bahr el

Ghazal, Equatoria and Upper Nile would run the country alternately, two terms of five years for each province, the old provinces to be renamed regions.

The party, say SPLM in a region such as say, Equatoria nominates a candidate for the party. The SPLM secretariats in the other two regions must support that candidate as their choice. The party supporters in all the other regions vote him/her into the office. The elected candidate forms a government of SPLM and he/she must run the country according to SPLM policies.

This system, I think, works in Nigeria. If the supporters of the party do not vote for their candidate, then it is the whole party which has lost the presidency. There should be no other candidates for the same positions in the other two regions. If a candidate still say from Equatoria, as the example above, leaves the office for any reason at all, including death, all his/her two terms are not completed, the vice president who might not be from Equatoria should complete the few months or years his/her predecessor left. In the next elections, the remaining term of five years should still go back to Equatoria by again nominating a new candidate for only one term.

The United Nations Secretary General is elected in this way. Each of the six continents get two terms of five years. It is very workable and very democratic. The present UN Secretary General is from Asia. He replaced an African Secretary General.

I think no region would reject the idea. Only if the head

of the state from that region does not govern the country well can the party secretariat from that region request his/ her replacement in the next term elections and put forward a new candidate to complete their tenure of office.

South Sudan is not mature politically including the so-called elites. It is the elites who are more divisive than those they think are uneducated. The elites do not appreciate democratic principles.

We are still tribalists, sectionalists and provincials. We question why the head of state comes from a particular region and not ours. We are not patient enough to wait. Everyone's term will come, no matter how long.

During the old days of Addis Ababa, Bahr el Ghazal Region did not rule the South but her people never complained. Bahr el Ghazal fought the liberation war whole heartedly but no one complained. A few from among us fell away from the SPLM/SPLA leadership.

The enemy bombarded Bahr el Ghazal heavily and devastated the region by using the Arab militia from Darfur and Kordofan. However, our people never faltered. Up to this day our young boys and young girls captured by the enemy during the war are still held in captivity and slavery by the Arabs militias.

Educated and learned persons who are very vocal against the large number of Dinka people in Juba should understand why. Even during the old school days our number was never surpassed by 'others' and 'they.' The proportion will always tilt in our favor. Using examinations as a means of filling vacant positions in the central government would be welcome. It would be somehow just and fair. However, in societies and communities like ours in South Sudan, corruption which has become endemic and incurable could be minimized if the examination results are adhered to by everyone in positions of authority.

Every authority that advertises a vacant position must abide by the conditions stipulated in the advertisement. He or she who is responsible for the selection of applicants should avoid the old formula of choosing by favoritism, tribalism, sectionalism and any other -*ism* not aforementioned. Competing by examination would encourage the young generation to read hard in order to pass and to improve their educational standard and qualifications. It would also force them to rely not on "who they know but what they know."

CHAPTER SIX

In visiting and evaluating our political and social set up one can fail to understand the direction we are taking. Dr. Garang's vision and manifesto have remained ink on paper. Dr. Garang was a socialist, a Sudanese nationalist who would have liked to rule the country under a circular constitution if the Muslims would have voted him into power.

However, many of us were separatists and we would have voted against one united Sudan. This is what we got after death robbed Dr. Garang of us. We got what we wanted. But do we and the leaders of SPLM follow Garang's vision? If it is all Garang's views and ideas then we should have projected them in all that we say and do in our offices and other institutions. There is nothing to show that at least we still remember what Dr. Garang preached.

The SPLM party is not active anywhere and in anything. However, the rank and file of supporters hear nothing useful but disputes, squabbles, quarrels and undermining one another among party leaders. Party rules and regulations which should be followed are ignored or thrown into the dustbin. At times the party leaders' communion boils down to tribal, provincial and sectional intrigues and squabbles which is very dangerous for a young nation. SPLM is dead. It is in the coffin, carried on the shoulders of the leaders and all shout at the top of their voices, *SPLM oyee, SPLM oyee*. All are searching for a burial plot. Dr. Garang Mausoleum will likely offer the ground.

I think that the socialist inspired institutions set up do not function properly in a multiparty system, as evidenced by special positions for youth and special seats for women in the party, legislature and government. Party workers' associations and civil defense or whatever name given to them should be part and parcel of a party.

When I search in my mind about what I know about multiparty systems, each party organizes itself in such a way that those institutions are accommodated within its set up. The women party activists, the youth activists etc. should rise to higher ranks within the party and not be privileged with special positions or seats.

The women's twenty-five or thirty-five percent representation in the legislature and government is unfair. Most women laud the percentage but who occupies the twenty-five or thirty-five percent among our women? Ninety-nine percent of our women are illiterate. The one percent who are literate are the wives and daughters of the present leaders in the government, the legislature and the civil service in the national institutions and the states.

The income accruing from the positions of both husbands and wives goes into one pot. It is either the husband who is in the assembly or government or vice versa, the wife. The majority of women who ululate or wail smell no flavor coming from the kitchens of women in high positions. Women should rise to higher echelons in the party and the government through their hard work, experience and popularity, as the men do.

Our youth may also claim representation as the women have done. However, my advice to the youth would be to first gain a good education and to progress steadily in whatever job assigned to you before jumping into politics. The present youth in the SPLM have not acquired a good education and the required experience. They regard the highly educated and experienced old people as rivals and enemies who should pass on rather than continue to tell them what they don't know and where they have gone wrong.

Education appears to carry no weight or importance in South Sudan. It is the highly educated and experienced people who are jobless, poor and regarded as enemies by those in positions of power.

The youth in high positions fail to manage the State's

affairs and the three "P's" well – Pleasure, Power and Pride. An educated and experienced old person puts the public interest and welfare first and foremost. He or she is honest, trustworthy and incorruptible. He or she wants to leave behind a good name for future generations to remember him or her by.

I do not have a problem with the youth climbing to higher positions. My point is, let them first acquire knowledge before being advanced to positions of power and authority. The youth now in the schools and universities do not study well. Why should they crave higher education when those with little or no education are members of the government and legislature? However, the richest South Sudanese are those who do not read and write.

I end this short article with words of wisdom from Socrates the ancient Greek philosopher concerning our youth: "Our youth love luxury, they have bad manners, contempt for authority, they show disrespect for their elders. They contradict their parents and tyrannize their teachers."

Lino Angok Kuec
Kuajok
April, 2013

ONE DAY SPENT UNDER THE BUSH

CHAPTER ONE

I t was a pitch-dark night, one June day in 1998. I heard the heavy foot traffic of both people and animals. Wave after wave of herds of cattle and people were rushing southward. It seemed the movement would never end. With all the heavy movement no other sound was heard. Both cattle and people hurried without speaking. I was puzzled but I knew that whenever there was a mass movement of people and cattle, it was to be inferred that the Arab enemy had come or was spending the night very near and they would probably raid the area at dawn. The whole population runs far deep inside the country with the cattle and young people. The Arabs' primary aim was to round up as many cattle as possible. The cattle would be sold by the raiders to enrich themselves and deprive the owners of their means of livelihood thus preventing the movement from continuing with the war. The SPLA soldiers depended on the local population for food. It was the same in 1986-1988 when the population withdrew far inside the country or migrated to the north during the great famine of those years.

The enemy's other purpose was to capture young people, boys and girls and other good looking young women. These were to be enslaved. The boys would look after the cows of the captors or other domestic animals, goats and sheep. The young women and girls would carry out domestic duties in the home becoming servants or be used to satisfy the male sexual urge. The women and girls also worked for free in the fields of their masters during the cultivation period. All were subjected to sale if the captor ran out of money.

The grown-up male and the old people both men and women and even the disabled were always killed. The area was to be cleared of the indigenous people so that it could be settled by Arabs. Whenever the Arab raiders entered a new area they would mark the trees and give it an Arab name so that they would have a right to claim it as their possession in the future. The Arab militia moved in groups of clans or sections. Whatever booty they collected was shared among themselves.

The foot movement was non-stop. The people came rushing according to the nearness of the distance to where I was in my home. The nearest villages to me were the first to pass by my house at midnight when they heard the signal. They were followed by village after village. The first villages where the first signal was sounded would be the last to arrive. Every time they came to a village it was found deserted and the escapees had to continue running in order to catch up with them. Those first villages would not stop running till they were sure the enemy was left far behind.

We were only four persons in my household; my young daughter who cooked for us, my old blind mother, the son of my sister who used to catch the stick of his blind grandmother to lead her, and myself. We had only one cow with its calf. We were a small family. I did not want to join the mass movement of people and animals.

The other members of my family were left in the Tonj area at the time I defected from Wau. I came alone to Twic to prepare a place of accommodation and something for the family to live on when they came to Twic. I had small children who would not be able to endure hunger and the frequent running and hiding from the Arab militias. Twic was in the front line and it had been devastated by the enemy since the inception of the movement in 1983.

I told my people to get ready and we would follow

when the rush of people and animals subsided. Morning hours were still far away. The enemy usually started their attack at six o'clock when it was relatively light. More and more people and cattle continued to rush by.

We remained alert for more than two hours before we started to follow. Two large wide tracks were made. The two were about three kilometers apart from each other with untrampled land between them. The tracks were so wide that the enemy could easily follow the people on horses and camels till they reached the places where the escapees settled. It would not matter how far or how many hours or days the people walked. The enemy would still find their hideout if nothing or no force stopped them from continuing with their parlous hunt. However, the buffer zone between the two tracks, about three kilometers wide, was untrampled and the trees and tall grass were untouched. The grass was luxuriously green and the trees were also green and leafy covered by climbers converging on the top of the trees.

Outside my house I entered the thick green untrampled grass and walked in it with my people and the cow followed by its calf. We walked in Indian file and made a thin line which an enemy in a hurry would not easily see. My idea was to avoid the tracks taken by both people and cattle.

After walking for two or three hours through the thick grass, we arrived at some very thick bush. The bush covered a wide area. Climbers were all over it up to the top of the trees, and it was dark underneath. As insufficient sunlight reached the ground, no grass or other vegetation grew under the canopy, but it was a little damp. The tracks made by the people and animals were to the east and west of us. No enemy would dare come here. The Arabs would only follow the cattle tracks. If any strayed they would not go more than a kilometer from the track to find them.

Our one cow and its calf settled down as soon as they were tethered to a tree branch, a makeshift stake as we were preparing to spread our plastic sheets on the ground. The cow and its calf understood that we were not moving any further. Each of us carried a plastic sheet to lie on and sleep on at night.

I had a light thin sponge mattress given to me by a Good Samaritan named Dan Eiff. Dan Eiff was an Irish man who led a group of journalists to Turalei. Mr. Eiff and his friends and accompanying pressmen came when our morale was at its lowest point, especially mine. They came either in March or April 1998. Dan Eiff and the journalists found me and others living under very harsh and appalling conditions. It was Dan Eiff and the pressmen's visit which enabled the International Community to learn about the looming famine in the whole of the Gogrial area in general and Twic County in particular. The enemy had terrorized Twic for many years. Dan's visit changed the terrible hunger situation in Twic and for me.

At the time of my arrival home, the Arab militia seized all my cattle together with those of my nearest relatives.

The cows for the bride price of my stepbrother's daughter were also taken. It was the cow which moved with me like a shadow that by chance remained behind. The cow was called *Yom* being the color Yom, that is brown all over its body and white at the forehead. For a bull or ox, it is *Mayom*. Yom had delivered a few days before the Arabs arrived and looted the cattle camps, which they found. The cow with me escaped from the Arabs. Its calf was left behind, either due to the heat or not being able to keep pace with the cattle being driven at full speed to the north. Not finding its calf nearby, Yom decided to return to the place they were driven from to search for its calf. The Arabs did not care about one cow escaping or going astray. Yom ran back and found its calf and so we also found it, after the enemy left the area.

I came to know Dan Eiff and he sympathized very much with my predicament, a university lecturer reduced to living in appalling conditions, worse than that of primitive man. He first offered me a large plastic tent which could accommodate the whole of my family.

When Dan Eiff and the journalists were leaving Turalei I went to bid them goodbye. Dan Eiff boarded the plane and brought out the sponge mattress and a very large woolen blanket. I had no words to thank him. I would have shed tears if I was not the man who had witnessed horrible atrocities in the past, such as the massacres of Gogrial and Wau in the years 1964 and 1965 respectively.

The Sudan Army and Fertit militia butchered the Dinka

and the Luo people in Wau in 1986-1988 as well as their nightly lynching of these tribes by the said army and the militia.

The Fertit had an old menace in their minds, which they repeated last year when they randomly and without cause, attacked and slaughtered, maimed and cut the Dinka and Luo bodies into pieces as if they were going to cook the flesh of those innocent men and women who lived among them. In those days the Fertit militia were free to butcher and to lynch the people of said tribes at will and to seek sanction and protection from the Sudan Government army. The Fertit were anti-movement and anti- the Dinka and Luo people.

In their insurgency against the Western Bahr el Ghazal government last year for no alleged reason except to massacre innocent people, the Fertit set alight the flag of South Sudan and raised up that of their old master al-Bashir. They even appealed to him to come to their aid. The learned and educated Fertit must have been mostly behind the move, to reject the transfer of Wau county to Bagara – the so-called 'learned and educated.' The Fertit and their leaders were not able to advise and to prevent their people from repeating the atrocities and barbarous acts of the past and to tell them that al-Bashir will never, never, never come to enslave South Sudan again.

A few Fertit who fought in the liberation war were targeted like Governor Rizzig Zacharia Hassan. The Fertit wanted to oust him out from the governorship, a position he earned through the ballot box let alone from the life he offered for the liberation of the country. He could have died like most of his colleagues who lay down their lives in the liberation struggle. But the good Lord spared his life and the position he now occupies should not be resented by people who were anti-movement and freedom. The Fertit who turned against him are those who received freedom on a platter. They got co-opted into the people's mass movement but they voted against the independence of South Sudan. However, they were tolerated. It is the same group who perpetrated the tribal violence. They are old guards and members of the former militia who are now clothed in SPLM skins, wolves in SPLM clothing.

The Fertit re-insurgency has reminded the people they had previously victimized to remember and to recall all the past atrocities and mass murder which they carried out during the war under the auspices of the Sudan Army and under their supervision and with the provision of arms and ammunition by the Sudan government army. Almost all the Fertit were generals and officers, both men and women in the militia.

The atrocities and genocide were forgiven, but not forgotten. But now the youth born during the war and who lost their parents and relatives at the hands of the Fertit militia are being reminded about the calamities of the recent past, the punishment meted out to their parents and relatives by the Fertit militia in collaboration with their old masters, the Arabs. There would be no reason to relate to the young generation the horrors and havoc of war meted out to their parents and relatives by our own brothers and sisters like the last which they witnessed or saw on the TV screens. Innocent people got killed and cut into pieces as if their flesh was going to be cooked and eaten.

CHAPTER TWO

I n an attack after Dan Eiff and his friends left and the members of the international press also left, the Arabs stole the tent. I was unable to carry it to where we ran to, so I hid it in one of the bushes but the enemy found it and carried it away. But I kept and prized the sponge mattress and the blanket. I parted with the two only when I left for the town after the signing of the CPA.

The thin light sponge mattress and the plastic sheet comforted me when I escaped to *dierkou*, the Sudd, with all the people of my village and area. I spent fourteen days on the Sudd by spreading the plastic sheet on the thin, soft soil of the Sudd and placing the sponge mattress on top of it when lying down or sleeping at night.

The Sudd is a very dangerous and inhospitable place.

It is infested with swarms of mosquitoes and other biting insects, amphibious animals and reptiles. I remained on the Sudd without cover from the scorching hot sun by day and the cold, dew and swarms of insects by night. A day or two on the Sudd and hunger began to bite the people, especially the children. The children cried throughout the day and night wanting something to eat but there was nothing to give them.

Some fathers and mothers ventured out of the Sudd area, in order to look for some wild fruits. Some succeeded and some were unlucky. The unlucky ones met their death at the periphery of the forest, killed by the enemy if they were men or taken captive and enslaved when they reached the north if they were women. The captured women were kept bound together, hand and foot, in the base camps of the Arab militia. They were to be marched to the north when the captors left.

Some brave women who were prepared to die rather than be taken captive were also killed. We tried to prevent the people from leaving the Sudd but hunger was severe. Some parents did not want to see their children starve to death while they were alive. Small children could not eat the bitter roots of the water lilies.

One day my young daughter and her stepbrother also ventured out despite my refusal to let them do so. They thought I was going to starve as I had refused to eat the bitter roots of the water lilies. The two children followed other big people towards the evening hours. The Arab raiders usually lifted their surveillance in the evening and returned to their main base camp five or six miles away intending to come again early next morning. My children and the other people with them expected the enemy to have gone, so they cautiously went out to look for the fruits of *cuei* – the tamarind tree and those of *tuk-bul* – the palm tree. These two types of trees had a lot of fruit on them. They crossed the last dry stream and were heading to a nearby forest in which these fruit trees were found in abundance when a few meters from the forest and the stream they saw several Arab raiders racing towards them at full speed on horseback. My young children could not keep up with the other grown-ups, the men, women, and the big boys and girls. All those older persons crossed the stream as fast as their long legs would carry them.

As my children could not manage to keep up with the others and they had delayed a little because they were apart from each other, they at first ran to find each other in order to escape together. After finding each other they started to run after the others. As luck would have it they crossed the stream before a horseman could catch either of them. One rider and his horse plunged into the stream bed. There was no water in the stream but the mud below the surface was soft. The horse got stuck and threw its rider. The man went headlong into the soft mud. He was badly hurt and unable to get up and run after the children. The other riders reined in their horses before reaching the stream bed. I think the Murahliin did not want to kill the children for reasons only God and they know. The Murahliin also did not see fit to alert their comrades who were keeping watch elsewhere for our people venturing out of the Sudd.

From that day forward I told my children to never attempt such a perilous venture again, at least until the enemy had left the area. They should learn to eat the bitter roots the people around us ate. I was not going to starve to death.

I think I ate a small tilapia in those fourteen days and no more. All around us was water, water and creeping plants, papyrus and elephant grass and a large number of amphibians. We all, especially the snakes and pythons, lived side-by-side.

A few months previous I had been a lecturer at the University of Bahr El-Ghazal and was now reduced to live in one of the most inhospitable places on earth, without shelter, food, clean drinking water and not even a concrete floor to put my head on. I had not a single piece of paper to show that I was once an academician. The clothes I had on me were as dirty as if I lived in a cesspool. The clothes and my sleeping things were infested with lice and other biting insects which made their home on them.

When the scorching hot sun poured down her rays I had to put up the thin mattress for cover. It could not prevent the sun's rays from penetrating through. I did not put up the blanket fearing that the wind might blow it into the water and I would have nothing to protect myself from the mosquitoes and the biting insects at night. If the blanket or the sponge mattress had fallen into the water, they would have absorbed water and it would have taken days for them to dry out. When I was able to bear the heat no longer I plunged into the abundant water all around me with all my filthy and stinking clothes on. The clothes had to dry on me also.

On the Sudd there are no trees which can provide shade for people, only tall elephant grass and papyrus which are in plentiful supply, but they have no dry soil underneath them so it is not possible to stay under them. *Dier*, or Sudd, is a moving and floating island. It can break up at any time and both parts drift apart. The whole population of my area had escaped to it and lived afloat upon it and I was with them.

Freedom has a price. It was a price paid in the pains, suffering and difficulties our people underwent since the inception of the war. Many of my people paid dearly with their lives not to mention the great wealth of cattle looted by the enemy and the number of women and children taken into slavery by the Arab militia.

The Fertit youth last year burned the South Sudan flag because they are not aware how freedom was achieved. They were very comfortable with the enemy and continued to be so after freedom was achieved. A person who underwent the difficulties and suffering brought about by the war would never think of touching that sacred object. He or she adores and reveres it. It is a symbol bought with the suffering and difficulties of millions and the loss of millions of lives.

The enemy spent fourteen days in the area. They set fire to every home, the grass and even fruit trees. They even lay dynamite under the trees which bear fruit such as mangoes, palm trees and even some tamarind trees and blew them up. The enemy did not want to leave anything edible for the people to turn back to when they left the area.

CHAPTER THREE

I emerged from the Sudd after fourteen days, unkempt and as listless as a leaf. I was on the verge of starvation. I could not walk steadily. The whole population which emerged from the Sudd was in the same pitiable and lamentable condition as me.

When another group of journalists and members of NGO's paid a visit to us at the periphery of the Sudd, they all wept. The whole community had to remain near the toc because there were no houses to return to. They were still littered with rotting human corpses so it was better to spend some days away from the horrible smell.

The journalists were accompanied by commander Salva Mathok Geng. When they arrived at the place where the people stayed none of them could imagine that a human being could live in such a horrible, deplorable and inhospitable place. I do not know what they would have done if they had found us on the Sudd a week before.

The visitors could not control their emotions. Every one of them burst into tears led by Commander Salva Mathok who picked up a starving child in his arms. Mathok wept bitterly like a child although he might have witnessed or seen worse situations like this one before.

I pitied commander Salva. Although he had witnessed worse situations than this yet he could not bear to see a starving child. Salva's behavior made me recall the scene which, it is reported, prompted a journalist to hang himself during the Rwanda genocide. The journalist came upon a three-year-old child crawling on all fours to a warehouse, or Rubb Hall, where he knew food was stored. There was nothing edible in the Rubb Hall or anywhere else the journalist looked to save the child's life. The journalist could not bear the scene. He was terribly traumatized. He went and killed himself by hanging.

Only two of us in the team did not weep, Awet Aken Atem the Payam Administrator of Aweng and me. The two of us lived and went through that horrible and lamentable situation. To our way of thinking things had improved. The enemy had left and the people were free to move about. They moved freely in search of whatever livelihood they could find to feed their starving children.

Staying on the Sudd and moving on it all the time, the water covers the sole and the toes of the foot. Remaining on it, something the Dinka call *nguendek* develops, that is, wounds develop between all the toes, in front of them and the sole. *Nguendek* cracks the skin all around the foot and causes a lot of pain, blistering and bleeding. It becomes very difficult to walk, either in the water, on grass or on dry land. *Nguendek* took weeks and even months for the wounds to heal. A person walks as if he or she is a leper.

CHAPTER FOUR

My old mother lay down without hesitation. Walking in the tall thick grass had exhausted her. She began to snore in no time. She did not close her eyes the whole night. Old people get some sleep towards dawn. It was cool and damp under the bush during the early hours of the morning. Then the mosquitoes began to attack and bite us so we set up a mosquito net around my mother.

The place around us became very quiet. The small birds we discovered in the bush and on the trees flew away when they realized that there were people inside the bush. When other small birds flew to the bush in search of fruits and insects they begin to chirp, then sensing or seeing us they also flew away. Many birds continued to come, twitter and then fly off. Apart from the noise made by the birds, the place was calm and quiet. The wind was still. Nothing stirred, neither human nor animal.

I was forced by want of knowledge to climb one of the tall trees in the middle of the bush. I pushed my head out of the creeper canopy and looked around especially to the east and west. I saw no people nor animals. This was when the enemy should have been moving, following the people and cattle, if they were around or if they had really come. Some other persons fleeing from the enemy's approach would have also appeared hurrying to places of safety. I wondered what was amiss. I surveyed the whole area up to where my eyes could reach on both sides. I could not see anything moving even in the grass which had not been trampled underfoot. I could not be seen as the climbers covered the top of other trees around me.

When I ascended a second time at about midday I saw a group of people returning to where we had escaped from last night. Those persons, more than ten of them, were walking back leisurely on the eastern side of the bush. Although it was hot they moved calmly. I could not tell whether they were soldiers or not. I remained sitting on the branch of the tree observing both sides. I also saw people going back on the western side walking in the same leisurely manner. Those people were nearer to me than those to the east. I recognized many of them. They were SPLA soldiers and some women carrying household utensils on their heads. They were returning to the same place we all ran from last night.

I descended the tree and went to them. Before I could ask them they told me to go back to the village. No Arab militia came. The people at Goknhom saw a soldier hurrying, riding a horse. Before the people could ascertain the identity of the rider, the first persons who saw him sounded the drums, signaling to the people that the Arabs had come. The signal went from village to village non-stop. It was that warning which prompted the whole population to run away with their children and cattle. It was difficult to cancel the signal once it had been sent. The signal was heard in all the villages and the people were already on the move. They knew the direction from which the signal came. When the soldier reached the fleeing people he pulled up his horse and told them not to panic and not run away. No enemy had come or was expected to come. The few persons the soldier stopped went back to their homes but most of the people and villages could not be reached, hence the great rush of the previous night. Two or three days ago there had been a battle between us and the enemy. The Arab militia attack was repulsed and some of their camels and horses were captured. The enemy retreated after having lost heavily both men and war materials. One of the captured horses was the one ridden by the soldier. The soldiers again asked me to take my people back to the village. I lived south of Wunrok and south of River Lol. They said,

'The people and cattle which ran away last night are coming back. All the people have been informed. It was a mistake but the people cannot be blamed. They should always be on the alert and prepared for any eventuality. The people should not rely on the few SPLA soldiers guarding the frontier. The few soldiers at the front could easily be overwhelmed by the mass of Arab militia whose number is always three to four times the number of the SPLA troops at the border. A small SPLA force can easily be overpowered and annihilated.'

I returned to where I left my people and related what the soldiers told me to my old mother. Before I could finish speaking we heard the sound of drums which are beaten when the cattle camp is being moved to a new location. The drum sounds as a signal to the bulls and oxen and other cattle. Almost all the big bulls follow the drummer closely. Most of the cows and oxen come behind. The suckling cows always come last as they wait to keep pace with their young calves. The calves by that time must have been tired having walked the whole night nonstop and at full speed.

My mother wanted us to leave at once but I told her to wait as we were not far from home. We had taken three hours to arrive under the bush because I left the track taken by the people and cattle. If the enemy had come they could have easily followed the large tracks and seized the cattle as they did last time. I took a different, difficult and awkward route. It was ours alone. An enemy in a hurry even if they had seen our track would have had no reason to take note of it. And there was nothing that might attract his attention. The grass we passed through was thick and a horse would not have been comfortable treading or running fast through it.

'The sun is hot. It is early afternoon. We shall move when it is cool in the evening. We shall walk to the nearest track, west of us and we shall reach our home before sunset,' I said.

I untied the cow and its calf and led them out of the bush to go and graze. My mother then asked my daughter to make her a cup of tea. We carried some sugar, tea and a box of matches. There was some water in a small jerry can. We usually kept water for my old mother. She was like a child and anything she needed was kept till she asked for it. After she had sipped two or three mouthfuls of tea she related to me a story from the past. She said to me, 'You did very well not to follow the route trampled underfoot by the rush of last night. You educated people learn easily from past mistakes.

'The enemy last time found our cattle because everybody ran in the same direction, people and cattle. All the cattle were rounded up, thousands and thousands of them. The Arabs had no more cause to search for the people. They became contented with the great booty that was before them. They left in a hurry fearing that the SPLA might amass troops to attack and prevent them from driving away their booty.

'During the slave trade and the Mahdiya,' she went back to the topic, 'whole villages moved in the same way the people did last night. The enemy was following them every time, using the tracks trampled underfoot by the people's movement. The people ran and ran as far away as they could go. They went and settled in the same hiding place. The enemy always followed their tracks and found them in a group after some time.

'The strong persons, men and women and other able-bodied persons escaped capture but their children and the old aged were rounded up and taken to slave camps. The disabled persons like me were either killed or left to die of hunger or eaten by wild beasts.

'Some women and their husbands foolishly returned when they saw their children crying and being manhandled and bound at the neck with others as if they were cattle. That foolish act aided the enemy to catch some strong and able-bodied persons and take them into slavery.

'The foolish mother and father failed to help their suffering children. They are all separated, men alone, women alone and children alone. The whole family is enslaved. They see each other suffering and in despair but without coming together again. The children are always the first to die of starvation and disease.

'At times a whole village was captured and marched away on foot in the thick forests, without food or rest to the slave centers. At those centers the slaves are sorted out. The young men and women and other able-bodied captives are exported to Arabland for sale.

'That situation went on for a long time but one day an

old wise man called all the inhabitants of his area together. He told them, "The enemy is finishing us. We must do something. As we are not able to fight them barehanded or with our heavy spears because the enemy has guns, from today onwards we shall not run in a group. A man, his wife and children should run and hide alone. If a family is unlucky and is caught, other families may be spared and be safe."

'That was also a time when wild animals were in great number, especially man-eaters or lions. People spent the nights in groups in the villages to protect themselves from the predators. However, everybody agreed with the old man's suggestion.

'When it was heard that the enemy was around or had actually arrived hunting for slaves, each family scattered in their own direction as you did with us today. The number of persons captured after that was greatly reduced.

'The old wise man's arrangement led to the famous Dinka saying *cuat meth wei, ku muk tony* – 'throw away the child and keep the pot.' The saying originated in the following way.

'An enemy came across a small family hiding, a man, his wife and their small child. The man carried their meagre sleeping things. By then these consisted of either a papyrus mat, a *yak* or cattle hide, a *biok weng*. The family usually hides but is ready to run when the enemy finds them. The man had folded the sleeping items and the woman had the child and the clay pot, the *tony tiop* near her. There were no pots made of iron in those days as they are today. The earthen pot is heavy and breakable. The child was also heavy and at the tender age of three or four years.

'When the enemy chanced upon their hiding place, the man picked up their sleeping things and ran. The woman took up the child and the clay pot and ran after her husband. The man ran in front followed by his wife with the child and the pot. The enemy followed them running in order to capture the woman with the child if they could not get the man. If the man foolishly returned as others before had done, then it was well and good.

'Suddenly the man came to a wide deep river full of water. He and his wife were good swimmers. The man stopped and urged his wife to increase her pace. When the woman caught up to her husband, the man jumped into the river with their meagre belongings. He ordered his wife to dive into the water. A fast enemy was drawing closer to her. When the woman came to the riverbank she discovered that she could not swim carrying both the clay pot and their child. She called to her husband and asked him, "What should I do with the child and the pot?" "Throw away the child and keep the pot!" the man shouted back.

'The woman did not hesitate. She threw away the child as directed by her husband and swam across the river carrying the pot. Both escaped capture. The Arabs are of short stature and almost none can swim across a river. The man and his wife were saved.

'That is how the Dinka people came to say when one is

in the tightest situation, *Cuat meth wei ku muk tony.* That is, make a decision even if one of the two sides are as dear to you as your child and your pot.

'The life of the man and his wife depended on the pot. They would not survive hiding if they had nothing to cook their food with. It was easier to find what to cook than finding a pot to cook it with. Fire could be made by striking two small sticks pressed against each other as is done today. The child would also die if the family had no means to cook food with or the child's cry would reveal their hiding place because a hungry child cries no matter what the parents say to it.

'Clay pots were not as common as they are today. Women clay pot makers were few and the village population was always on the move to avoid the slave hunters and their Dinka collaborators. (The Arabs had hired *mounyjieng cin puoth*, Dinkas without heart to catch their kith and kin and hand them over to the enemy. Those Dinka men became more dangerous than their Arabs masters.) If a family broke their earthen pot, it took weeks or even months to procure another one. Clay pots were acquired through bartering and the potters would not fire an earthen pot if the price was not settled immediately. It could take months or even a year for a buyer and the potter to meet if the price was not paid at the beginning of the sale. The price of the pot was usually paid in kind, dura, dry fish or tobacco.

'People kept moving from place-to-place hiding from the slavers. The people would cook in one place, move to another place to eat there and then walk a distance in order to spend the night there. The people used to cook at night and hide during the daytime. Smoke from a fire could be seen from far away and the enemy would run to it especially their local agents for the Arabs had appointed and armed many Dinka collaborators to do the dirty work for them besides the hired ones.

'It was not possible for many families to use one cooking pot. Who could wait the whole night before the earthen pot was emptied? Water does not boil quickly in a clay pot and it takes many hours before a clay pot is hot. One must put a lot of firewood under an earthen pot to get it boiling and too much heat can easily break it. So, the man and his woman would not have survived if they had thrown away their earthen pot.'

Lino Angok Kuec
Kuajok, Warrap State, South Sudan
February, 2013

INDEX

Normandy 221
Nuer 3, 172, 187-9, 191-2, 197-201
Nur 94
Nuul 185-186, 190-4, 197, 201, 203-210
Nyala 150
Nyaraweng 198
Nyasaland 218
Nyerere 217
Nyigat 162, 165, 167-172
Nyin 152
Nyok 118
Obote 217-218
Okello 216
Omar 226
Pacific 220
Pampas 220
Panacier 161-162
Patrice 219
Payam 265
Payams 171
Pibor 187
Pio 113, 125, 133-4, 138, 140-1, 146-7
Platoon 45
Prairies 220
Raga 12, 80, 85-7, 89, 98, 106, 124-5

Rainwater 60
Raja 44
Rek 198
Rhodesia 218
Riak 18, 20-1, 23
Riau 169
Richard 145
Riel 1, 3-4, 6-8, 10, 13-5, 17, 40, 45-7, 49-51, 56-7, 59, 63-70, 72, 75, 78, 81-2, 88-90, 93, 100-1, 103, 105, 108-9, 125, 128-9, 131-3, 140, 151-3
Riir 180-184
Riverside 118
Rizzig 255
Robert 218
Roman 219
Rual 230
Rubb 265
Rumbek 1-3, 12, 15, 17-22, 38, 114, 119, 168
Russia 220
Russian 98
Rwanda 265
Sahara 220
Salva 116, 264-5
Samaritan 200, 204, 253

LINO ANGOK KUEC